Genius
Sudoku

Cardoza
Publishing

Arnold
Snyder

Go online to cardozapublishing.com to enjoy other challenging sudoku and puzzle books.

Cardoza Publishing is the foremost gaming and gambling publisher in the world with a library of almost 200 up-to-date and easy-to-read books and strategies. These authoritative works are written by the top experts in their fields and with more than 11 million books in print, represent the best-selling and most popular gaming books anywhere.

ISBN 13: 978-1-58042-393-9

Visit our website for a full list of gambling, gaming and puzzle books

CARDOZA PUBLISHING
www.cardozapublishing.com

INTRODUCTION

The puzzles in this book are all difficult to solve by Sudoku standards. Sure, they're not the simplest challenges in the world—and yes, you'll have to strain your brain to work them out—but you can solve all of them using basic logic with no guesswork required.

Each Sudoku here is new with a unique personality all its own. That's because, unlike a lot of authors, I don't use computer programs to generate my Sudoku. I personally handcraft all of my puzzles to give you plenty of challenges with a special flair that you won't find anywhere else.

Listing candidates for empty cells will prove quite useful in working these puzzles. True geniuses may not need to use this method, but most ordinary people may be unable to solve many of the sudoku in this book without using it to fill the empty cells. If you don't know how to use the candidate technique, I give a full explanation of it in *Sudoku Formula 2*, along with an added *bonus*—my own method of using "key numbers" for empty cells, something you won't find in any other book.

If you enjoy even more difficult challenges, you'll also want to get my book, *Sadistic Sudoku*. And you'll find complete instructions on how to solve the most difficult expert-level puzzles you'll find anywhere in my book, *Sudoku Formula 3*. In fact, the instructional sections of my three-book *Sudoku Formula* series will teach you how to solve even the toughest puzzles—*fast*.

Put on your thinking caps and start solving these 200 brand new puzzles I've designed for *genius-level* puzzlers like you—all created by hand to give your brain a real workout. Have fun!

PUZZLES

1

3								9
		6			8	5		1
1	2		7					
	9	1						3
			5		3			
2						4	8	
					5		4	8
6		5	3			9		
9								7

2

			9		7	3	6	
	1					5		
		2	1					
	6	4			5	1		
			8		3			
		5	7			9	3	
					9	6		
		3					7	
	8	9	6		4			

3

		6	9					5
						1		7
3		1			4			
9	7							
4			6	2	9			3
							9	4
			5			7		6
1		4						
2					1	8		

4

	2	5						
1	7		6				5	
	8		7		9	4		
				8		5	9	
	9	3		4				
		9	5		6		4	
	5				3		8	1
						6	7	

5

	1				8	9	5	
4	6				7			
7			3				6	
	9	6						
				5				
						2	4	
	4				6			1
			7				8	9
	2	5	8				3	

6

	1			3			8	
5		9			6	4		
	6			8	2			
4			3			9		
		2			9			1
			8	9			1	
		5	1			6		9
	7			4			5	

7

9			8	4				
	1	2			9			
					1	7		
7			9					8
4		5				6		9
1				7				3
		4	1					
			6			2	4	
			3	8				1

8

						6	2	
		3					9	1
	9					3	5	
			9	8			4	
	6		1		4		8	
	5		7	6				
	8	5					2	
6	1					8		
		7	3					

9

	2		8				7	
					2			5
	3				5	2		
4	5			1		7		
9								8
		8		4			6	1
		6	3				5	
7			9					
	1				7		2	

10

7					4			9
	6				2			
			8		6			
			5				8	7
		2				4		
9	3				6			
		1		3				
			1				2	
8			7					5

11

8				1			3	
1		9					7	
	5	4		8	7			
			6					1
	3						5	
6					8			
			1	7		2	9	
	4					3		6
	8			9				5

12

			3				1	8
3		9		6		4		
			8			5		3
	7		5					
5								1
					3		4	
1		3			4			
		8		9		6		2
7	9				8			

13

		1	2				6	
		5	8					4
				9	4		5	
8				6			3	
			5		9			
	7			8				2
	1		4	5				
2					1	3		
	5				6	8		

14

	1	5			6			2
						3	7	5
7				5		1		
			5					
		9		1		5		
				4				
		2		9				3
6	4	7						
5				7			8	6

15

				7		8	1	
			3		4			6
				1		4		
	4		9			2		
9	3						6	8
		2			8		3	
		1		5				
3			8		7			
	6	5		2				

16

	7		8		4		9	
	6		9					
3								8
		7			1			3
	5	9				8	6	
8			4			5		
7								6
					6		5	
	1		3		8		2	

17

1			6					
	7			2	9	3		
5		3			7			
			7			4	3	
			9		3			
	5	1			6			
			2			9		1
		2	4	7			8	
					1			4

18

1			7				2	
			6	1			8	5
						7	4	
	5				3	9		
		1	5		6	2		
		7	8				3	
	2	9						
8	4			6	9			
	7				4			

19

1	6				4		8	3
			7					
		8		9				
		5	1				2	
2		4				7		1
	8				9	3		
				5		1		
					3			
8	3		4				5	6

20

1								
9	7				4	1	5	
	8					7		
5			8		2		7	
7		3				5		8
	6			5		9		1
		7					6	
	3	8	1				4	2
								7

21

		3						8
4			2		6	1		
					4	3		
	1			6				4
			1		8			
5				9			2	
		9	5					
		2	7		1			6
1						8		

22

			8		2			6
	8			3	9			7
						4		9
	9				7		3	
2								8
	1		5				9	
6		2						
8			9	5			4	
5			3		4			

23

	1						8	2
							5	3
		7	5		1			4
5	3			8				
				7				
				3			4	5
8			4		9	6		
4	7							
6	9						2	

24

	1	3		8	4		7	
			3					
		9						
	4	1	9					7
	2		5		7		6	
3					1	9	8	
						5		
					2			
	8		7	6		2	1	

25

		1						7
3		9	7					
	2				6	8		
		4	8			5		
	6			2			9	
		5			1	7		
		8	5				7	
					3	2		4
9						6		

26

	2	9	1	8				
		5						
1				9	3			
2			9				1	3
9								4
3	1				7			6
			3	6				7
						8		
				7	4	5	3	

27

		1			6		4	
	7			5	8			
		2	4					
6		8					9	
		7	5		3	2		
	4					6		3
					7	3		
			8	9			2	
	1		6			5		

28

	5	8					3	
4							6	
		6	9	5				
	3	5						
1			5	2	6			3
						7	5	
				9	4	1		
	2							7
	7					4	8	

29

	6						7	5
7		5	6				1	8
			9					
9				2	5			
4								1
			8	6				3
			7					
5	9				8	3		2
2	3						8	

30

7			4		1			8
		8		2		7		
6			8		7			1
		1				8		
2			6		4			3
		5		9		3		
3			1		6			4

31

		3			8	9		
	2		9			3		
		4			7			8
	9			7				6
			5		3			
4				1			8	
5			2			8		
		6			9		4	
		9	3			7		

32

8	6				9		2	7
		5		4				
3						9		
4			6	1		2		
		3		5	7			6
		4						2
				8		3		
6	9		7				4	5

33

2	7					3		
			8				1	7
8		9			5			2
		5						
			6	9	3			
						6		
9			5			2		8
5	3				1			
		4					3	1

34

3								9
	5	2		1		3	4	
4	1						2	6
			3		7			
	8						5	
			9		1			
2	3						8	7
	7	9		2		6	3	
6								5

35

							3	5
		4	7		2			8
	6					2		4
	7							3
		8		1		7		
5							2	
8		9					1	
2			3		8	6		
4	5							

36

					6	3		
	2		9			8		1
	7	8		3				4
			3		1	7		
		1	2		8			
5				2		9	3	
8		4			5		6	
		6	8					

37

				2			3	8
3	1						7	
5	8		6			9		
			2					5
		9				8		
7					1			
		6			2		5	4
	3						1	6
4	7			3				

38

3							8	
	6	5					7	1
			3	6			4	9
			6			1		
5	3						2	7
		7			8			
7	5			1	4			
8	9					7	1	
	1							3

39

	6							
		3	1	8			4	
	7				2			1
	3			6	5		8	
		8				5		
	1		2	3			9	
7			8				2	
	2			4	3	7		
							1	

40

6	4				1	5		7
	3							
	8				6	2		
3	5					8		
	1	8					5	7
			2				1	8
			6	8			4	
							2	
7				4	2		8	6

41

9				6		8	7	
4		2			9		5	
		5	4					
			7		3	1		
		3	6		4			
				5	7			
	6		8			4		3
	1	4		7				2

42

2	7			3				1
		3			6	2		
			5	4			8	
	4	1						
	6						1	
						8	3	
	3		7	8				
		6	9			1		
8				2			4	5

43

	9			3		6		
				5	2	8		
	2		4					
1			7					8
8		6				1		4
4					3			6
					4		7	
		4	5	1				
		5		2			6	

44

		6	9			3		4
3					7			
					2		9	
	5	9		8				
		8	2		3	6		
				5		7	1	
	4		5					
			3					1
5		3			1	2		

45

	2		5			9		
	3				1			
	5			6				
		5			3	4		
	8		6	9	4		3	
		9	8			7		
				4			5	
			9				6	
		2			8		1	

46

8		6				7		
								4
			7	9	1			5
				2	4	6		
		4	1		8	9		
		1	9	3				
2			8	7	5			
6								
		3				4		2

47

							2	5
				3				
	5	4	9	7				
4					3		1	7
5	7						9	2
6	1		5					8
				4	2	1	3	
				1				
7	9							

48

	2		5			6		
5					3			
			2	1			9	3
			9					6
1			8		4			2
8					1			
4	8			3	7			
			1					7
		1			9		8	

49

9		5						
		7			1			
6	3		4			1		
	6		2					5
4								6
2					9		3	
		8			5		2	3
			3			6		
						4		9

50

1	4				9			8
				3				6
		6			7	4		
						2		9
	7			4			1	
5		8						
		2	3			6		
9				5				
6			8				3	2

51

8	4							
				6		8	5	
			9				2	
	4		2	5		3		
	3			4		6		
	5			8	9	7		
	2				5			
	5	6		7				
							9	1

52

			2	5			7	4
					1		2	
				6				
	1	9				8		
7			4	2	5			3
		2				7	6	
				4				
	6		9					
4	5			7	8			

53

	4				5	3		9
	7				9	2		
	2				4			1
9				1				7
2				5				4
6			7				8	
		7	2				9	
3		8	5				6	

54

9		4	6					
					7	5	2	
			1					
8						4	1	
7	1						3	9
	5	2						8
					6			
	8	9	3					
					9	7		6

55

						4	8	9
					7			6
		4	2					5
7	6		5					
1		5				3		8
					8		6	7
5					3	2		
6			7					
9	3	1						

56

		2						7
6					3	2		
				7		5		4
8			9			3	4	
3								6
	5	7			6			1
9		3		1				
		6	8					2
2						7		

57

		3		9			7	8
8								
9				6	8		5	
		7					6	
		5	2		6	4		
	1					8		
	3		1	2				5
								3
2	5			4		1		

58

3	4	1	2					
5	6		1	8			3	
1		9	3			5		
		7			8	4		2
	2			5	1		9	3
					3	7	2	4

59

					9	5	4	
	5	7	6					
						7		
	9	1	3				5	
	3		1		4		6	
	7				5	1	9	
		9						
					6	8	2	
	1	3	2					

60

6			4		5			
			9	3				7
							5	2
9		7				2		
		2				1		
		1				6		3
2	3							
1				7	6			
			8		3			1

61

					3			
				1			2	7
	4	1			9	6		
			6	1	8	9		
	8						1	
	1	4	5	8				
		7	3			2	6	
3	5			4				
			2					

62

	8			5			3	
		6	4					1
3				6	2			7
		7						
			7	9	4			
					3			
8			1	2				3
1					3	6		
	5			7			4	

63

	5				4		8	
9		6			1			2
						9		4
				6		7		
		5		7		3		
		8		1				
7		2						
3			7			4		9
	8		3				2	

64

1								4
		7			2	5		6
6	9		8					
	4	6						1
			5		1			
9						3	2	
					5		3	2
7		5	1			4		
4								8

65

			4		8	1	7	
	6					5		
		9	6					
	7	3			5	6		
			2		1			
		5	8			4	1	
					4	7		
		1					8	
	2	4	7		3			

66

		7	4					5
						6		8
1		6			3			
4	8							
3			7	9	4			1
							4	3
			5			8		7
6		3						
9					6	2		

67

	9	5						
6	8		7				5	
	2		8		4	3		
				2		5	4	
	4	1		3				
		4	5		7		3	
	5				1		2	6
						7	8	

68

	6				2	4	5	
3	7				8			
8			1				7	
	4	7						
				5				
						9	3	
	3				7			6
			8				2	4
	9	5	2				1	

69

	6			1			2	
5		4			7	3		
	7			2	9			
3			1			4		
		9			4			6
			2	4			6	
		5	6			7		4
	8			3			5	

70

	3				1		7	
4		9						3
			6				4	
		2		6				5
	6		2		8		3	
8				7		1		
	9				4			
7						3		6
	1		3				9	

71

					7	9		
		1					4	6
	4					1	5	
				4	2		3	
	7		6		3		2	
	5		8	7				
	2	5					9	
7	6					2		
		8	1					

72

	9		2				8	
					9			5
	1			5	9			
3	5			6		8		
4								2
		2		3			7	6
		7	1				5	
8			4					
	6				8		9	

73

4		7	1	9				
		9		6				
5			4	3				
	5					6	3	
		1				5		
	4	2					8	
				4	8			3
				2		9		
				5	6	1		4

74

2				6			1	
6		4					8	
	5	3		2	8			
			7					6
	1						5	
7					2			
			6	8		9	4	
	3					1		7
	2			4				5

75

			1				6	2
1		4		7		3		
		2			5		1
	8		5					
5								6
					1		3	
6		1			3			
		2		4		7		9
8	4				2			

76

		6	9				7	
		5	2					3
				4	3		5	
2				7			1	
			5		4			
	8			2				9
	6		3	5				
9					6	1		
	5				7	2		

77

	6	5			7			9
						1	8	5
8				5		6		
			5					
		4		6		5		
					3			
		9		4				1
7	3	8						
5			8			2	7	

78

				8		2	6	
			1		3			7
				6		3		
	3		4			9		
4	1						7	2
		9			2		1	
		6		5				
1			2		8			
	7	5		9				

79

	8		2		3		4	
	7		4					
1								2
		8			6			1
	5	4				2	7	
2			3			5		
8								7
					7		5	
	6		1		2		9	

80

				7		8	4	5
					1		7	
7		5	8			9		
		7						8
	8	4				6	3	
2						1		
		1			3	4		6
	3		1					
6	7	9		4				

81

			8				9	
			7	6			2	5
						8	3	
	5				1	4		
		6	5		7	9		
		8	2				1	
	9	4						
2	3			7	4			
	8				3			

82

6	7				3		2	1
			8					
		2		4				
		5	6				9	
9		3				8		6
	2				4	1		
				5		6		
					1			
2	1		3				5	7

83

4					6		5	
			7	5		1	3	
					1			2
		5					6	7
		2				4		
1	7					5		
8			5					
	2	6		9	3			
	5		4					9

84

		1						2
3			9		7	6		
					3	1		
	6			7				3
			6		2			
5				4			9	
		4	5					
		9	8		6			7
6					2			

85

			2		9			7
	2			1	4			8
						3		4
	4				8		1	
9								2
	6		5				4	
7		9						
2			4	5			3	
5			1		3			

86

	6						2	9
							5	1
		8	5		6			3
5	1			2				
				8				
				1			3	5
2			3		4	7		
3	8							
7	4						9	

87

	6	1		2	3		8	
			1					
		4						
	3	6	4					8
	9		5		8		7	
1					6	4	2	
						5		
					9			
	2		8	7		9	6	

88

		6						8
1			4	8				
	9				7	2		
		3	2			5		
	7			9			4	
		5			6	8		
		2	5				8	
					1	9		3
4						7		

89

	9	4	6	2				
		5						
6				4	1			
9			4				6	1
4								3
1	6				8			7
			1	7				8
						2		
			8	3	5	1		

90

5			2				7	
	2			4				6
		9				4		
8			3			1		
	9			1			3	
		1			9			8
		5				9		
1				7			2	
	8				6			3

91

	5	2					1	
3							7	
		7	4	5				
	1	5						
6			5	9	7			1
						8	5	
				4	3	6		
	9							8
	8					3	2	

92

	7						8	5
8		5	7				6	2
			4					
4				9	5			
3								6
			2	7				1
				8				
5	4				2	1		9
9	1						2	

93

				7	4			
5				2		7		9
1								5
	3			6			1	2
		2				4		
8	6			3			5	
9								1
2		7		1				3
			7	8				

94

		1			2	4		
	9		4			1		
		3			8			2
	4			8				7
			5		1			
3				6			2	
5			9			2		
		7			4		3	
		4	1			8		

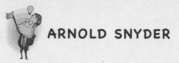

95

2	7				4		9	8
		5		3				
1						4		
3			7	6		9		
		1		5	8			7
		3						9
				2		1		
7	4		8				3	5

96

9	8					1		
			2				6	8
2		4			5			9
		5						
			7	4	1			
						7		
4			5			9		2
5	1				6			
		3					1	6

97

5	7							
	2		1	8				
	8		6				1	3
9		2						1
			8		3			
3						7		2
1	6				4		3	
			3	1			2	
							5	9

98

4							6	
6								9
1				6	8	2		
8		6	5	1				
	7						5	
				8	3	9		6
		9	2	7				3
7								8
	2							4

99

				3		5	6	1
3	5				4			
			2					
9		1		4				
4			8		6			9
				7		3		6
				8				
			7				3	4
8	2	7		6				

100

	1		7		9			
								8
		7	2		3			1
	6					4	8	
				5				
	9	2					6	
9			3		6	7		
3								
			1		7		4	

101

	8	2		4	6	3		
6			5					7
			9			1		
						9	3	1
9	6	4						
		6			9			
1					2			9
		3	8	1		5	2	

102

					5			2
7			1	4			3	
				8	4	9		
4		7						
5								1
					7			5
	9	1	7					
	2			6	4			8
6			3					

103

	5		3			4		
8	3		1	7				2
						1		
				8		7	1	5
9	2	7		1				
		5						
2				9	1		8	6
		4			6		2	

104

		5				4		
4	9			3			2	1
	1	6				9	3	
			4		7			
	2						8	
			5		3			
	8	7				1	4	
6	4			1			7	5
		2				6		

105

	4	2						
		8	7		1			9
1		9					6	
		4					7	
7				3				8
	1					2		
	3					8		5
6			4		8	1		
						9	2	

106

4					6			
8		3	5				1	
		9		4			7	8
7			4		3			
			1		8			3
5	4			1		2		
	6				2	8		9
			8					6

107

	4	8		1				
	7					4	3	
5			6			2	8	
		2	1					
8								5
					3	7		
	2	9				1		6
	3	6					4	
				4		9	7	

108

	8					4		
	7	3					6	2
	9	5	4	6				
3			6					
	1	7				2	4	
					8			7
				3	9	7	2	
7	3					8	5	
		4					3	

109

							6	
	9		3	8				4
		3			1		7	
	8			6	2		4	
2								8
	5		1	4			3	
	1		8			7		
7				9	4		1	
	3							

110

3				4				6
				2	7			
		2				8		
			5		6		8	
5	1						3	4
	2		1		4			
		8				4		
			3	9				
6				5				9

111

2	5			3		9		
	7				9	4		6
		4						7
1			5		8			
			3		4			8
5					7			
4		8	2				3	
		6		5			1	4

112

		1		8		6	5	
6					3			8
	2			7	4			
							4	1
	1						3	
2	8							
			5	2			8	
1			9					3
	4	7		6		2		

113

3				8			9	
2				7	6			
			4				6	
		2	5			1		
1		4				2		3
		3			8	4		
	5				4			
			7	1				4
	3			6				7

114

8		4	9					3
					5	8		
	9				6			
				2			7	9
3			6		8			2
5	1			7				
			7				4	
			1	8				
6					1	7		8

115

9			7				6	
					1		8	
				3			7	
4					8			7
	8		3	9	4		2	
5			2					9
	7			4				
	3		9					
	1				2			6

116

5						2		3
		4						
		7	5	9	1			
3				6	4			
9			1		2			4
			9	8				1
			2	5	7	6		
						3		
4		6						8

117

	6	7						
				8				
			9	5			7	4
	1	5			8	4		
	9	6				7	5	
		2	7			3	1	
1	8			4	6			
				1				
						5	9	

118

3			7				6	
					8	7		
	9	8	6	1				
		3	9					
		6	2		4	1		
					1	2		
				8	5	4	2	
		5	1					
	2				9			1

119

						9		7
					1			5
1			4			3	8	
		7	6				3	
		3				4		
	8				9	6		
	6	8			7			2
3			8					
4		9						

120

8			9			6	2	
9						7	3	
	5							
3				9			7	
			8		5			
	2			6				3
							8	
	8	6						1
	4	7			3			2

121

						2	4	
2	7			3				
	6		9					
8			6	7				4
3				4				8
5				2	9			7
					7		6	
				5			7	3
	9	1						

122

	5	4	6	7				
	6				1			
				3				
2							1	9
		8	4	6	7	5		
5	3							6
				4				
			9				3	
				5	2	4	7	

123

8		9			7		4	
6					9		5	
		1			4		6	
		5		1		9		
		4		7		6		
	2		5			3		
	9		6					5
	3		7			8		2

124

			3			9		4
7	6				5			
			1					
4	1					2		
	8	9				5	1	
		2					7	6
					3			
			8				2	9
5		3			9			

125

4	2	9						
		3			5			
		7	6					4
			7			5	3	
8		2				1		7
	3	5			2			
6					8	7		
			5			3		
						9	8	1

126

		5						6
6					8	3		
7		4		5				
8	4		9			2		
		3				8		
		1			3		7	5
				1		9		8
		6	2					3
5						6		

127

	5	2		9				8
						2		
	7			3	2	9		
	3							5
4			6		3			7
2							1	
		7	1	6			8	
		8						
1				4		6	7	

128

			6			8	4	1
	8		1	2		7	3	
7			8			1		9
4		6			2			5
	9	8		7	1		6	
5	6	4			8			

129

7	4				9			
			3				7	5
5								
	7		8				9	1
	3		1		4		8	
1	9				7		5	
								9
2	6				3			
			6				1	8

130

				1			7	
7	2					6		
	6		7	8	2		4	
				6	8		5	
4								7
	8		4	9				
	7		6	5	4		2	
		2					6	5
	1			2				

131

					8			
	6	5		1				
3					9		4	1
2	9			3	1			
	1						2	
			7	2			1	4
6	3		8					5
				4		8	7	
			6					

132

	8			7			2	
		1	4					3
		5		3	6	8		
								5
			5	9	4			
8								
		8	1	6		2		
3					8	1		
	4			5			7	

133

	2				4		7	
		6			1	9		3
9		4						
5				3				
8				5				7
				1				2
						5		6
4		9	5			8		
	6		8				2	

134

		4				1		
7		3			6			5
		2				3	9	
		1					4	3
			7		1			
8	6					9		
	8	6			7			
4			1			5		7
		2				4		

135

1	5		4		2			
7							3	
			3					9
3					7		5	8
			6		1			
4	1		2					7
5					4			
	2							1
			5		8		6	4

136

	7	4				5

		7	4					5
3		2						
					8	1		3
						4	2	
		1	5	9	4	8		
	4	8						
2		5	7					
						3		8
6					3	9		

137

							9	7
	7		5			3	2	
8			2		4		6	
7	4			6				
				8			4	1
	8		7		5			4
	6	3			1		7	
5	2							

138

4	7				6		3	
					2	8	5	
	5		1			2		
							4	5
				7				
9	8							
		3			5		8	
	6	4	2					
	1		6				9	7

139

	6			1			3	
8					5	7		4
				6	9		5	
4			1			8		
	3			4				9
	3		6	4				
5		4	3					7
	7			8			2	

140

			7		9			
		4				7	5	3
2	1				6	9		
		1					2	
9		3				6		4
	2					3		
		4	3				9	2
3	7	9			2			
			6		4			

141

9					5			
	4	3						1
1	7						4	
	8			4	6			
	6		3		8		5	
			2	5			7	
	9						6	7
6						5	3	
			1					2

142

	2		6				9	
		7			9			
9					7		1	
2				3		8	7	
		6				4		
	5	3		8				6
	7		1					5
			4			2		
	9				2		3	

143

			1	9		4		5
				3				9
			4	8		7		
3	8						7	
7								1
	2						4	6
		8		4	2			
9				6				
1		4		7	3			

144

	1			3		6		
	2					3		4
				6	2		7	8
		3	5					
	7						1	
					6	5		
9	4		3	2				
1		5					8	
		7		4			6	

145

	3	6	1					
8				5		1		4
7		1	6					
			7				2	
		3				7		
	8				1			
					8	3		1
5		9		4				6
					6	2	4	

146

	5		9					3
		8	6					7
	7			4	8			
	1			5		6		
			7		4			
		9		6			2	
			8	7			3	
1					3	9		
6					5		7	

147

		9			5		3	7
1	2	7						
3				7		2		
			7					
7				3				4
					8			
		1		4				9
						5	8	2
6	5		2			7		

148

6	3			2				
		5	1		8			
8				3				
9			4				8	
	5	6				4	1	
	1				6			9
				7				3
			6		2	1		
				9			5	7

149

	4		6		8		2	
			4				5	
		6				1		
		1			3			2
6	5						7	4
7			8			6		
		5				2		
	7				5			
	9		1		6		3	

150

	2			6		3		
					7			9
6			1					
		4			3		8	
9								6
	3		8			2		
					2			1
7			6					
		1		8			9	

151

	9		2					
	6	7	5	3				
2	8							
4					1		7	
9			7		5			3
	1		6					2
							9	4
				5	4	6	8	
				8		2		

152

	6	1			8	3	5	
			2					
				4				6
	9		3					7
2		3				9		8
1					4		6	
3				7				
					1			
	7	5	8				6	1

153

	7				3	4		
1	8		5	7				
		6			1			
	3	5						7
4								6
7						1	5	
			7			2		
				9	8		6	3
		9	4				7	

154

		6						1
3			9		5	8		
1					8			
		8		5			3	
			3		6			
	9			4		7		
			7					4
		5	2		3			9
6						3		

155

		5	6		9			
		2		1	4		6	
8		4						
	1				2		4	
		6				9		
	4		7				3	
						5		9
	8		4	7		6		
			1		8	7		

156

	6	9					3	
	7	1						
		8	7		3			2
				6		7	1	
				2				
	8	7		1				
5			8		4	6		
						8	2	
	9					5	4	

157

	2			6	8		3	1
			1					
								4
		2	4				8	3
	5		7		2		9	
4	6				3	1		
7								
					9			
9	3		2	5			6	

158

		2						3
			2			1		4
6				5		9		
7			6					8
	4			9			5	
2				3				7
	2		7					6
9		8			1			
5						4		

159

			3	6			9	4
								7
				4	1	3		
	3	1	4			9		
		8				4		
		5			2	1	3	
		2	1	5				
6								
7	1			2	8			

160

	1	6						
5			8				3	
3	7				4		9	
	6	3	4				2	
		5		2		9		
	9				8	3	1	
	5		1				4	3
	3				7			6
						5	7	

161

	1						7	6
	5					8		
			4	7				5
							1	7
		1	7	9	5	3		
2	7							
3				4	8			
		2					9	
8	6						2	

162

	2	7					5	
	3	6	5			2		7
				4				
				9	7	4		
		3				8		
		1	6	5				
				2				
1		9			6	7	4	
	6					9	1	

163

				5	4			
5		9		6		7		
		7				1		
	1	6		3			8	
4								6
	7			8		2	3	
		1				9		
		8		1		6		5
			5	2				

164

4					6			1
1			4				9	
		6			2			8
		5		2			4	
			7		1			
	6			3		8		
6			9			7		
	8				4			5
2			1					4

165

	9	2			4	6	5	
				8				7
4						1		
9			5	3		8		
		5		7	2			1
		9						8
1				6				
	8	7	2			5	4	

166

1						9	2	
	3	2	6					
		9			7	6		4
								7
			5	4	1			
5								
9		6	7			4		
					3	7	1	
	1	3						8

167

						7	5	
			1	2			6	
	1	8	3				2	
		1				9		6
			2		8			
5		6				8		
	8				4	1	3	
	6			8	1			
	7	9						

168

	3					4		
		9				3		
6				3	2	1		
			7	1		2		3
	7						5	
9		3		2	8			
		8	6	5				9
		2				5		
		4				6		

169

7	3	1		8				
				4	8	7		
			6					
				4		9		1
		9	2		3	4		
8		3		5				
					2			
	8	4	5					
				3		2	6	5

170

		2	5		7		4	
1			8	2		9	5	
	3	7						4
		1				7		
9						2	6	
	9	6		1	8			2
	4		2		6	3		

171

8				4	3		2	6
		5	7			3		
1			9					
9	8	1						
						9	3	4
					9			3
		9			6	1		
7	6		2	1				8

172

		6			7			
	8		1	4		5		
4	9				2			
						4		5
		1				7		
5		7						
			5				9	1
		2		3	4		6	
			8			3		

173

4			8				7	
		6	1	5		2	8	
1								
5	1	7		2				
				1		9	6	5
								7
	2	3		9	1	6		
	6				3			4

174

	8	1				7	3	
9	3			7			1	4
		5				9		
			3		1			
	5						8	
			4		2			
		4				3		
3	6			2			5	7
	7	9				6	2	

175

	2					8		4
9			3		8	7		
						6	5	
		3					1	
1				2				8
	7					5		
	3	5						
		8	1		7			6
7		6					9	

176

4	3			7		5		
	9				5	8		6
			8					9
1			3		2			
			7		8			2
3					9			
8		2	4				7	
		6		3			1	8

177

	5	6			7			9
	2	9					3	
				3		6	1	
		5	7					
8								4
					2	1		
	3	8		7				
	1					3	2	
4			9			5	8	

178

				2	6	1	5	
1	2					8	4	
		3					2	
2			9					
	7	1				5	3	
					8			1
	8					3		
	1	2					9	5
	6	4	3	9				

179

	7		8			1		
1				6	3		7	
	2							
	8			9	5		3	
5								8
	4		7	3			2	
							9	
	6		2	8				3
		2			7		1	

180

	5		9					3
1					2		7	8
				6	8			
		3		1		4		
	9		3		7		8	
		1		5		3		
			6	8				
8	3		2					5
9					3		2	

181

4					1			
3		8	5				2	
		9		4			7	3
7			4		8			
			2		3			8
5	4			2		6		
	1				6	3		9
			3					1

182

			4	5			8	
7			6					2
	3	1		9		5		
							3	7
	7						2	
5	8							
		7		8		9	4	
9					2			8
	5			1	3			

183

	4				3			
			1	7				3
	2			9				1
		5	4			7		
7		3				5		2
		2			8	3		
2				8			6	
5				1	9			
			3				9	

184

			1				3	
		7	8					
9					7	1		8
				5			1	6
2			9		8			5
4	7			1				
8		3	6					2
					4	8		
	6				9			

185

	1			3				
	2		6					
	7				5			9
3					8			1
	8		2	6	3		5	
4			5					6
6			1				9	
					7		8	
				2			1	

186

			5	4	1	9		
						2		
3		9						8
2				9	3			
6			7		5			3
			6	8				7
4						5		2
		3						
		1	4	6	7			

187

7	8			3	9			
				7				
							4	6
	7	4			8	3		
	6	9				1	4	
		5	1			2	7	
	9	1						
				8				
			6	4			1	3

188

2				8	4	3	5	
		4	7					
	5				6			7
		2	6					
		9	5		3	7		
					7	5		
2			1				9	
					8	1		
	6	8	9	7				

189

	9	8			1			5
2			8					
3		6						
		1	9				2	
		2				3		
	8				6	9		
						6		1
				7				4
7			3			2	8	

190

			5			9		
				4	8		2	
			7				6	8
3	4	5		1				6
	9						1	
6				5		4	9	2
1	7			8				
	3		1	2				
		6			3			

191

					1		9	
				4			1	2
	6	7						
8			9	1				3
2				3				8
4				5	6			1
						5	3	
5	1			2				
	9		6					

192

				3				
			6				2	
				4	5	3	1	
5							7	6
		8	3	9	1	4		
4	2							9
	4	3	9	1				
	9				7			
				2				

193

	5		4			2		
	6		9					4
	2		1			8		5
	4			7		6		
	3			1		9		
8		6			1		3	
9					6		4	
		7			3		9	

194

					2			
			8				5	6
4		2			6			
3	7					5		
	8	6				4	7	
		5					1	9
			2			6		3
1	9				4			
			7					

195

9					8	1		
			4			2		
						6	8	7
			1			4	2	
8		5				7		1
	2	4			5			
3	5	6						
		2			4			
		1	9					3

196

				7		6		8
		9	5					2
4						9		
8	3		6			5		
		2				8		
		7			2		1	4
		4						9
9					8	2		
1		3		4				

197

		1	7	9			8	
		8						
7				3		9	1	
	2							4
3			9		2			1
5							7	
	4	5		6				8
						5		
	1			2	5	6		

198

	6	8		1	7		9	
4	9	3			8			
1			8			7		6
3		9			5			4
			9			8	3	7
	8		7	5		1	2	

199

								6
5	9				2			
			9				7	8
	1		8				6	7
	2		7		3		8	
7	6				1		4	
1	3				6			
			2				1	4
4								

200

		2	8				5	
9							2	
						7	3	9
	5			4		2	6	
		1		6		3	5	
		8		5		1		7
8	2	4						
	6							5
	9				6	3		

SOLUTIONS

1

3	5	8	4	1	2	7	6	9
4	7	6	9	3	8	5	2	1
1	2	9	7	5	6	8	3	4
5	9	1	8	6	4	2	7	3
8	4	7	5	2	3	1	9	6
2	6	3	1	7	9	4	8	5
7	1	2	6	9	5	3	4	8
6	8	5	3	4	7	9	1	2
9	3	4	2	8	1	6	5	7

2

4	5	8	9	2	7	3	6	1
7	1	6	4	3	8	5	9	2
9	3	2	1	5	6	7	4	8
3	6	4	2	9	5	1	8	7
1	9	7	8	6	3	4	2	5
8	2	5	7	4	1	9	3	6
2	7	1	3	8	9	6	5	4
6	4	3	5	1	2	8	7	9
5	8	9	6	7	4	2	1	3

3

7	8	6	9	1	3	4	2	5
5	4	9	2	8	6	1	3	7
3	2	1	7	5	4	9	6	8
9	7	2	4	3	5	6	8	1
4	1	8	6	2	9	5	7	3
6	3	5	1	7	8	2	9	4
8	9	3	5	4	2	7	1	6
1	6	4	8	9	7	3	5	2
2	5	7	3	6	1	8	4	9

4

9	2	5	8	1	4	7	3	6
1	7	4	6	3	2	8	5	9
3	8	6	7	5	9	4	1	2
2	6	1	3	8	7	5	9	4
5	4	8	9	6	1	3	2	7
7	9	3	2	4	5	1	6	8
8	1	9	5	7	6	2	4	3
6	5	7	4	2	3	9	8	1
4	3	2	1	9	8	6	7	5

5

3	1	2	4	6	8	9	5	7
4	6	8	5	9	7	3	1	2
7	5	9	3	1	2	8	6	4
5	9	6	2	8	4	1	7	3
2	7	4	1	5	3	6	9	8
1	8	3	6	7	9	2	4	5
8	4	7	9	3	6	5	2	1
6	3	1	7	2	5	4	8	9
9	2	5	8	4	1	7	3	6

6

2	1	7	9	3	4	5	8	6
5	8	9	7	1	6	4	2	3
3	6	4	5	8	2	1	9	7
4	5	8	3	6	1	9	7	2
1	9	6	2	7	8	3	4	5
7	3	2	4	5	9	8	6	1
6	2	3	8	9	5	7	1	4
8	4	5	1	2	7	6	3	9
9	7	1	6	4	3	2	5	8

7

9	5	7	8	4	6	1	3	2
3	1	2	7	5	9	8	6	4
6	4	8	3	2	1	7	9	5
7	2	3	9	6	4	5	1	8
4	8	5	2	1	3	6	7	9
1	6	9	5	8	7	4	2	3
5	9	4	1	7	2	3	8	6
8	3	1	6	9	5	2	4	7
2	7	6	4	3	8	9	5	1

8

5	4	1	9	3	6	2	7	8
8	7	3	4	5	2	6	9	1
2	9	6	8	1	7	3	5	4
1	3	2	5	9	8	7	4	6
7	6	9	1	2	4	5	8	3
4	5	8	7	6	3	9	1	2
3	8	5	6	4	9	1	2	7
6	1	4	2	7	5	8	3	9
9	2	7	3	8	1	4	6	5

9

5	2	9	8	3	4	1	7	6
1	8	4	7	6	2	9	3	5
6	3	7	1	9	5	2	8	4
4	5	3	6	1	8	7	9	2
9	6	1	2	7	3	5	4	8
2	7	8	5	4	9	3	6	1
8	9	6	3	2	1	4	5	7
7	4	2	9	5	6	8	1	3
3	1	5	4	8	7	6	2	9

13

9	4	1	2	3	5	7	6	8
6	3	5	8	1	7	9	2	4
7	8	2	6	9	4	1	5	3
8	9	4	7	6	2	5	3	1
1	2	3	5	4	9	6	8	7
5	7	6	1	8	3	4	9	2
3	1	9	4	5	8	2	7	6
2	6	8	9	7	1	3	4	5
4	5	7	3	2	6	8	1	9

10

7	8	5	6	1	4	2	3	9
3	6	4	9	5	2	8	7	1
2	1	9	3	8	7	6	5	4
1	4	6	5	2	3	9	8	7
5	7	2	8	9	1	4	6	3
9	3	8	4	7	6	5	1	2
4	5	1	2	3	8	7	9	6
6	9	7	1	4	5	3	2	8
8	2	3	7	6	9	1	4	5

14

8	1	5	3	7	6	4	9	2
9	2	6	4	8	1	3	7	5
7	3	4	2	5	9	1	8	6
4	7	1	5	6	3	9	2	8
2	6	9	8	1	7	5	3	4
3	5	8	9	2	4	6	1	7
1	8	2	6	9	5	7	4	3
6	4	7	1	3	8	2	5	9
5	9	3	7	4	2	8	6	1

11

8	7	6	4	1	9	5	3	2
1	2	9	5	6	3	8	7	4
3	5	4	2	8	7	1	6	9
7	9	2	6	3	5	4	8	1
4	3	8	9	2	1	6	5	7
6	1	5	7	4	8	9	2	3
5	6	3	1	7	4	2	9	8
9	4	7	8	5	2	3	1	6
2	8	1	3	9	6	7	4	5

15

4	5	6	2	7	9	8	1	3
1	7	9	3	8	4	5	2	6
2	8	3	6	1	5	4	9	7
6	4	8	9	3	1	2	7	5
9	3	7	5	4	2	1	6	8
5	1	2	7	6	8	9	3	4
7	9	1	4	5	6	3	8	2
3	2	4	8	9	7	6	5	1
8	6	5	1	2	3	7	4	9

12

6	4	5	3	2	7	9	1	8
3	8	9	1	6	5	4	2	7
2	1	7	8	4	9	5	6	3
9	7	4	5	1	2	3	8	6
5	3	2	4	8	6	7	9	1
8	6	1	9	7	3	2	4	5
1	2	3	6	5	4	8	7	9
4	5	8	7	9	1	6	3	2
7	9	6	2	3	8	1	5	4

16

1	7	2	8	3	4	6	9	5
5	6	8	9	1	7	2	3	4
3	9	4	6	2	5	7	1	8
6	2	7	5	8	1	9	4	3
4	5	9	2	7	3	8	6	1
8	3	1	4	6	9	5	7	2
7	4	5	1	9	2	3	8	6
2	8	3	7	4	6	1	5	9
9	1	6	3	5	8	4	2	7

17

1	2	9	6	3	4	8	5	7
8	7	4	5	2	9	3	1	6
5	6	3	1	8	7	2	4	9
6	9	8	7	1	2	4	3	5
2	4	7	9	5	3	1	6	8
3	5	1	8	4	6	7	9	2
4	3	5	2	6	8	9	7	1
9	1	2	4	7	5	6	8	3
7	8	6	3	9	1	5	2	4

21

7	2	3	9	1	5	4	6	8
4	8	5	2	3	6	1	7	9
6	9	1	8	7	4	3	5	2
9	1	7	3	6	2	5	8	4
2	4	6	1	5	8	7	9	3
5	3	8	4	9	7	6	2	1
8	6	9	5	4	3	2	1	7
3	5	2	7	8	1	9	4	6
1	7	4	6	2	9	8	3	5

18

3	1	5	7	4	8	6	2	9
7	9	4	6	1	2	3	8	5
6	8	2	9	3	5	7	4	1
2	5	8	4	7	3	9	1	6
4	3	1	5	9	6	2	7	8
9	6	7	8	2	1	5	3	4
5	2	9	1	8	7	4	6	3
8	4	3	2	6	9	1	5	7
1	7	6	3	5	4	8	9	2

22

9	5	7	8	4	2	3	1	6
1	8	4	6	3	9	5	2	7
3	2	6	1	7	5	4	8	9
4	9	8	2	1	7	6	3	5
2	6	5	4	9	3	1	7	8
7	1	3	5	6	8	2	9	4
6	4	2	7	8	1	9	5	3
8	3	1	9	5	6	7	4	2
5	7	9	3	2	4	8	6	1

19

1	6	7	5	2	4	9	8	3
9	2	3	7	6	8	5	1	4
4	5	8	3	9	1	6	7	2
3	7	5	1	4	6	8	2	9
2	9	4	8	3	5	7	6	1
6	8	1	2	7	9	3	4	5
7	4	6	9	5	2	1	3	8
5	1	2	6	8	3	4	9	7
8	3	9	4	1	7	2	5	6

23

9	1	5	6	4	3	7	8	2
2	6	4	7	9	8	1	5	3
3	8	7	5	2	1	9	6	4
5	3	6	9	8	4	2	7	1
1	4	8	2	7	5	3	9	6
7	2	9	1	3	6	8	4	5
8	5	2	4	1	9	6	3	7
4	7	3	8	6	2	5	1	9
6	9	1	3	5	7	4	2	8

20

1	4	5	7	2	3	6	8	9
9	7	2	6	8	4	1	5	3
3	8	6	9	1	5	7	2	4
5	9	1	8	3	2	4	7	6
7	2	3	4	6	1	5	9	8
8	6	4	5	7	9	2	3	1
4	1	7	2	9	8	3	6	5
6	3	8	1	5	7	9	4	2
2	5	9	3	4	6	8	1	7

24

5	1	3	2	8	4	6	7	9
8	7	4	3	9	6	1	2	5
2	6	9	1	7	5	8	3	4
6	4	1	9	2	8	3	5	7
9	2	8	5	3	7	4	6	1
3	5	7	6	4	1	9	8	2
7	9	2	8	1	3	5	4	6
1	3	6	4	5	2	7	9	8
4	8	5	7	6	9	2	1	3

25

6	8	1	2	5	4	9	3	7
3	5	9	7	1	8	4	2	6
4	2	7	3	9	6	8	5	1
2	1	4	8	7	9	5	6	3
7	6	3	4	2	5	1	9	8
8	9	5	6	3	1	7	4	2
1	4	8	5	6	2	3	7	9
5	7	6	9	8	3	2	1	4
9	3	2	1	4	7	6	8	5

29

3	6	9	2	8	1	4	7	5
7	2	5	6	4	3	9	1	8
8	1	4	5	9	7	2	3	6
9	8	3	1	2	5	6	4	7
4	5	6	7	3	9	8	2	1
1	7	2	8	6	4	5	9	3
6	4	8	3	7	2	1	5	9
5	9	7	4	1	8	3	6	2
2	3	1	9	5	6	7	8	4

26

4	2	9	1	8	6	3	7	5
8	3	5	7	4	2	6	9	1
1	7	6	5	9	3	4	2	8
2	6	4	9	5	8	7	1	3
9	5	7	6	3	1	2	8	4
3	1	8	4	2	7	9	5	6
5	8	2	3	6	9	1	4	7
7	4	3	2	1	5	8	6	9
6	9	1	8	7	4	5	3	2

30

7	5	2	4	6	1	9	3	8
9	3	4	5	7	8	6	1	2
1	6	8	9	2	3	7	4	5
6	9	3	8	5	7	4	2	1
5	4	1	2	3	9	8	6	7
2	8	7	6	1	4	5	9	3
4	1	5	7	9	2	3	8	6
8	2	6	3	4	5	1	7	9
3	7	9	1	8	6	2	5	4

27

9	5	1	3	2	6	8	4	7
4	7	6	9	5	8	1	3	2
3	8	2	4	7	1	9	5	6
6	3	8	2	1	4	7	9	5
1	9	7	5	6	3	2	8	4
2	4	5	7	8	9	6	1	3
5	2	9	1	4	7	3	6	8
7	6	3	8	9	5	4	2	1
8	1	4	6	3	2	5	7	9

31

6	1	3	4	2	8	9	5	7
7	2	8	9	6	5	3	1	4
9	5	4	1	3	7	6	2	8
1	9	5	8	7	4	2	3	6
8	6	2	5	9	3	4	7	1
4	3	7	6	1	2	5	8	9
5	7	1	2	4	6	8	9	3
3	8	6	7	5	9	1	4	2
2	4	9	3	8	1	7	6	5

28

7	5	8	6	4	1	2	3	9
4	9	2	3	8	7	5	6	1
3	1	6	9	5	2	8	7	4
2	3	5	4	7	9	6	1	8
1	8	7	5	2	6	9	4	3
6	4	9	8	1	3	7	5	2
8	6	3	7	9	4	1	2	5
5	2	4	1	6	8	3	9	7
9	7	1	2	3	5	4	8	6

32

8	6	1	5	3	9	4	2	7
9	7	5	2	4	1	6	3	8
3	4	2	8	7	6	9	5	1
4	5	9	6	1	8	2	7	3
7	8	6	3	9	2	5	1	4
2	1	3	4	5	7	8	9	6
1	3	4	9	6	5	7	8	2
5	2	7	1	8	4	3	6	9
6	9	8	7	2	3	1	4	5

33

2	7	6	9	1	4	3	8	5
4	5	3	8	2	6	9	1	7
8	1	9	3	7	5	4	6	2
6	9	5	7	4	8	1	2	3
1	2	7	6	9	3	8	5	4
3	4	8	1	5	2	6	7	9
9	6	1	5	3	7	2	4	8
5	3	2	4	8	1	7	9	6
7	8	4	2	6	9	5	3	1

37

9	6	7	1	2	4	5	3	8
3	1	4	8	5	9	6	7	2
5	8	2	6	7	3	9	4	1
6	4	3	2	8	7	1	9	5
1	2	9	3	4	5	8	6	7
7	5	8	9	6	1	4	2	3
8	9	6	7	1	2	3	5	4
2	3	5	4	9	8	7	1	6
4	7	1	5	3	6	2	8	9

34

3	6	7	2	4	8	5	1	9
9	5	2	7	1	6	3	4	8
4	1	8	5	3	9	7	2	6
1	9	4	3	5	7	8	6	2
7	8	3	4	6	2	9	5	1
5	2	6	9	8	1	4	7	3
2	3	5	6	9	4	1	8	7
8	7	9	1	2	5	6	3	4
6	4	1	8	7	3	2	9	5

38

3	7	9	4	5	1	6	8	2
4	6	5	8	9	2	3	7	1
2	8	1	3	6	7	5	4	9
9	2	8	6	7	3	1	5	4
5	3	6	1	4	9	8	2	7
1	4	7	5	2	8	9	3	6
7	5	3	9	1	4	2	6	8
8	9	4	2	3	6	7	1	5
6	1	2	7	8	5	4	9	3

35

7	8	2	4	6	1	9	3	5
3	9	4	7	5	2	1	6	8
1	6	5	8	3	9	2	7	4
6	7	1	2	8	4	5	9	3
9	2	8	5	1	3	7	4	6
5	4	3	9	7	6	8	2	1
8	3	9	6	2	5	4	1	7
2	1	7	3	4	8	6	5	9
4	5	6	1	9	7	3	8	2

39

2	6	1	3	5	4	8	7	9
9	5	3	1	8	7	2	4	6
8	7	4	6	9	2	3	5	1
4	3	2	9	6	5	1	8	7
6	9	8	4	7	1	5	3	2
5	1	7	2	3	8	6	9	4
7	4	5	8	1	6	9	2	3
1	2	9	5	4	3	7	6	8
3	8	6	7	2	9	4	1	5

36

4	5	9	1	8	6	3	2	7
6	2	3	9	4	7	8	5	1
1	7	8	5	3	2	6	9	4
9	4	2	3	5	1	7	8	6
7	8	5	4	6	9	2	1	3
3	6	1	2	7	8	5	4	9
5	1	7	6	2	4	9	3	8
8	3	4	7	9	5	1	6	2
2	9	6	8	1	3	4	7	5

40

6	4	2	8	1	5	9	3	7
5	3	1	7	9	4	8	6	2
9	8	7	3	6	2	4	5	1
3	5	6	1	7	8	2	9	4
2	1	8	9	4	6	5	7	3
4	7	9	2	5	3	6	1	8
1	2	3	6	8	9	7	4	5
8	6	4	5	3	7	1	2	9
7	9	5	4	2	1	3	8	6

41

9	3	1	5	6	2	8	7	4
4	7	2	1	8	9	3	5	6
6	8	5	4	3	7	2	1	9
8	2	6	7	9	3	1	4	5
1	4	9	2	5	8	6	3	7
7	5	3	6	1	4	9	2	8
2	9	8	3	4	5	7	6	1
5	6	7	8	2	1	4	9	3
3	1	4	9	7	6	5	8	2

45

1	2	6	5	8	7	9	4	3
9	3	8	4	2	1	6	7	5
7	5	4	3	6	9	1	8	2
6	1	5	2	7	3	4	9	8
2	8	7	6	9	4	5	3	1
3	4	9	8	1	5	7	2	6
8	9	3	1	4	6	2	5	7
5	7	1	9	3	2	8	6	4
4	6	2	7	5	8	3	1	9

42

2	7	5	8	3	9	4	6	1
4	8	3	1	7	6	2	5	9
6	1	9	2	5	4	7	8	3
3	4	1	5	6	8	9	2	7
7	6	8	3	9	2	5	1	4
9	5	2	4	1	7	8	3	6
1	3	4	7	8	5	6	9	2
5	2	6	9	4	3	1	7	8
8	9	7	6	2	1	3	4	5

46

8	9	6	4	5	3	7	2	1
1	7	5	2	8	6	3	9	4
4	3	2	7	9	1	8	6	5
9	8	7	5	2	4	6	1	3
3	2	4	1	6	8	9	5	7
5	6	1	9	3	7	2	4	8
2	4	9	8	7	5	1	3	6
6	1	8	3	4	2	5	7	9
7	5	3	6	1	9	4	8	2

43

5	9	7	8	3	1	6	4	2
3	4	1	6	5	2	8	9	7
6	2	8	4	7	9	3	1	5
1	3	2	7	4	6	9	5	8
8	7	6	2	9	5	1	3	4
4	5	9	1	8	3	7	2	6
2	8	3	9	6	4	5	7	1
9	6	4	5	1	7	2	8	3
7	1	5	3	2	8	4	6	9

47

1	3	7	4	6	8	9	2	5
9	8	6	2	3	5	4	7	1
2	5	4	9	7	1	8	6	3
4	2	8	6	9	3	5	1	7
5	7	3	1	8	4	6	9	2
6	1	9	5	2	7	3	4	8
8	6	5	7	4	2	1	3	9
3	4	2	8	1	9	7	5	6
7	9	1	3	5	6	2	8	4

44

8	2	6	9	1	5	3	7	4
3	9	5	8	4	7	1	6	2
1	7	4	6	3	2	8	9	5
7	5	9	1	8	6	4	2	3
4	1	8	2	7	3	6	5	9
6	3	2	4	5	9	7	1	8
2	4	1	5	6	8	9	3	7
9	6	7	3	2	4	5	8	1
5	8	3	7	9	1	2	4	6

48

9	2	3	5	4	8	6	7	1
5	1	6	7	9	3	2	4	8
7	4	8	2	1	6	5	9	3
3	5	4	9	7	2	8	1	6
1	6	7	8	5	4	9	3	2
8	9	2	3	6	1	7	5	4
4	8	5	6	3	7	1	2	9
2	3	9	1	8	5	4	6	7
6	7	1	4	2	9	3	8	5

SOLUTIONS

49

9	1	5	8	2	6	3	4	7
8	4	7	9	3	1	5	6	2
6	3	2	4	5	7	1	9	8
7	6	3	2	8	4	9	1	5
4	8	9	5	1	3	2	7	6
2	5	1	7	6	9	8	3	4
1	9	8	6	4	5	7	2	3
5	7	4	3	9	2	6	8	1
3	2	6	1	7	8	4	5	9

53

1	4	6	8	2	5	3	7	9
5	7	3	1	6	9	2	4	8
8	2	9	3	7	4	6	5	1
9	3	4	6	1	8	5	2	7
7	8	5	4	3	2	9	1	6
2	6	1	9	5	7	8	3	4
6	1	2	7	9	3	4	8	5
4	5	7	2	8	6	1	9	3
3	9	8	5	4	1	7	6	2

50

1	4	7	5	6	9	3	2	8
8	9	5	4	3	2	1	7	6
3	2	6	1	8	7	4	9	5
4	6	3	7	1	5	2	8	9
2	7	9	6	4	8	5	1	3
5	1	8	9	2	3	7	6	4
7	8	2	3	9	4	6	5	1
9	3	1	2	5	6	8	4	7
6	5	4	8	7	1	9	3	2

54

9	7	4	6	2	5	3	8	1
3	6	1	8	9	7	5	2	4
5	2	8	1	4	3	9	6	7
8	9	3	7	6	2	4	1	5
7	1	6	4	5	8	2	3	9
4	5	2	9	3	1	6	7	8
2	4	7	5	1	6	8	9	3
6	8	9	3	7	4	1	5	2
1	3	5	2	8	9	7	4	6

51

8	4	2	5	1	7	9	6	3
1	3	9	4	6	2	8	5	7
5	6	7	9	3	8	1	2	4
7	8	4	2	5	6	3	1	9
2	9	3	7	4	1	6	8	5
6	1	5	3	8	9	7	4	2
3	2	1	8	9	5	4	7	6
9	5	6	1	7	4	2	3	8
4	7	8	6	2	3	5	9	1

55

2	7	6	3	1	5	4	8	9
3	5	9	4	8	7	1	2	6
8	1	4	2	6	9	7	3	5
7	6	8	5	3	4	9	1	2
1	2	5	9	7	6	3	4	8
4	9	3	1	2	8	5	6	7
5	8	7	6	4	3	2	9	1
6	4	2	7	9	1	8	5	3
9	3	1	8	5	2	6	7	4

52

1	9	8	2	5	3	6	7	4
6	3	4	7	9	1	5	2	8
2	7	5	8	6	4	1	3	9
5	1	9	6	3	7	8	4	2
7	8	6	4	2	5	9	1	3
3	4	2	1	8	9	7	6	5
9	2	7	5	4	6	3	8	1
8	6	3	9	1	2	4	5	7
4	5	1	3	7	8	2	9	6

56

5	9	2	4	6	8	1	3	7
6	7	4	1	5	3	2	8	9
1	3	8	2	7	9	5	6	4
8	6	1	9	2	7	3	4	5
3	2	9	5	4	1	8	7	6
4	5	7	3	8	6	9	2	1
9	4	3	7	1	2	6	5	8
7	1	6	8	3	5	4	9	2
2	8	5	6	9	4	7	1	3

57

5	6	3	4	9	1	2	7	8
8	7	4	5	3	2	9	1	6
9	2	1	7	6	8	3	5	4
4	9	7	8	1	3	5	6	2
3	8	5	2	7	6	4	9	1
6	1	2	9	5	4	8	3	7
7	3	8	1	2	9	6	4	5
1	4	9	6	8	5	7	2	3
2	5	6	3	4	7	1	8	9

61

6	7	5	4	2	3	1	8	9
8	3	9	6	1	5	4	2	7
2	4	1	8	7	9	6	5	3
5	2	3	7	6	1	8	9	4
7	8	6	9	3	4	5	1	2
9	1	4	5	8	2	7	3	6
4	9	7	3	5	8	2	6	1
3	5	2	1	4	6	9	7	8
1	6	8	2	9	7	3	4	5

58

3	4	1	2	7	9	6	5	8
9	7	8	6	3	5	2	4	1
5	6	2	1	8	4	9	3	7
1	8	9	3	4	2	5	7	6
2	5	4	7	1	6	3	8	9
6	3	7	5	9	8	4	1	2
7	2	6	4	5	1	8	9	3
4	9	3	8	2	7	1	6	5
8	1	5	9	6	3	7	2	4

62

7	8	2	9	5	1	4	3	6
5	9	6	4	3	7	8	2	1
3	4	1	8	6	2	5	9	7
4	2	7	3	1	5	9	6	8
6	3	8	7	9	4	2	1	5
9	1	5	2	8	6	3	7	4
8	6	4	1	2	9	7	5	3
1	7	9	5	4	3	6	8	2
2	5	3	6	7	8	1	4	9

59

3	8	2	7	1	9	5	4	6
1	5	7	6	4	2	3	8	9
9	6	4	5	8	3	7	1	2
2	9	1	3	6	7	4	5	8
5	3	8	1	9	4	2	6	7
4	7	6	8	2	5	1	9	3
8	2	9	4	7	1	6	3	5
7	4	5	9	3	6	8	2	1
6	1	3	2	5	8	9	7	4

63

1	5	7	9	2	4	6	8	3
9	4	6	8	3	1	5	7	2
8	2	3	6	5	7	9	1	4
2	3	9	5	6	8	7	4	1
4	1	5	2	7	9	3	6	8
6	7	8	4	1	3	2	9	5
7	9	2	1	4	5	8	3	6
3	6	1	7	8	2	4	5	9
5	8	4	3	9	6	1	2	7

60

6	7	3	4	2	5	8	1	9
5	2	8	9	3	1	4	6	7
4	1	9	6	8	7	3	5	2
9	6	7	3	1	8	2	4	5
3	5	2	7	6	4	1	9	8
8	4	1	5	9	2	6	7	3
2	3	4	1	5	9	7	8	6
1	8	5	2	7	6	9	3	4
7	9	6	8	4	3	5	2	1

64

1	5	2	3	6	9	8	7	4
3	8	7	4	1	2	5	9	6
6	9	4	8	5	7	2	1	3
5	4	6	2	7	3	9	8	1
2	3	8	5	9	1	6	4	7
9	7	1	6	8	4	3	2	5
8	6	9	7	4	5	1	3	2
7	2	5	1	3	8	4	6	9
4	1	3	9	2	6	7	5	8

SOLUTIONS

65

3	5	2	4	9	8	1	7	6
8	6	7	3	1	2	5	4	9
4	1	9	6	5	7	8	3	2
1	7	3	9	4	5	6	2	8
6	4	8	2	7	1	3	9	5
2	9	5	8	3	6	4	1	7
9	8	6	1	2	4	7	5	3
7	3	1	5	6	9	2	8	4
5	2	4	7	8	3	9	6	1

69

9	6	8	4	1	3	5	2	7
5	2	4	8	6	7	3	9	1
1	7	3	5	2	9	6	4	8
3	5	2	1	7	6	4	8	9
6	4	7	9	8	2	1	3	5
8	1	9	3	5	4	2	7	6
7	9	1	2	4	5	8	6	3
2	3	5	6	9	8	7	1	4
4	8	6	7	3	1	9	5	2

66

8	2	7	4	6	1	3	9	5
5	3	4	9	2	7	6	1	8
1	9	6	8	5	3	4	7	2
4	8	9	3	1	5	7	2	6
3	6	2	7	9	4	5	8	1
7	1	5	6	8	2	9	4	3
2	4	1	5	3	9	8	6	7
6	7	3	2	4	8	1	5	9
9	5	8	1	7	6	2	3	4

70

6	3	5	4	9	1	2	7	8
4	2	9	5	8	7	6	1	3
1	8	7	6	3	2	5	4	9
9	7	2	1	6	3	4	8	5
5	6	1	2	4	8	9	3	7
8	4	3	9	7	5	1	6	2
3	9	6	7	2	4	8	5	1
7	5	4	8	1	9	3	2	6
2	1	8	3	5	6	7	9	4

67

4	9	5	2	6	3	8	1	7
6	8	3	7	1	9	2	5	4
1	2	7	8	5	4	3	6	9
9	7	6	1	2	8	5	4	3
5	3	2	4	7	6	1	9	8
8	4	1	9	3	5	6	7	2
2	6	4	5	8	7	9	3	1
7	5	8	3	9	1	4	2	6
3	1	9	6	4	2	7	8	5

71

5	3	6	4	1	7	9	8	2
2	8	1	3	5	9	7	4	6
9	4	7	2	6	8	1	5	3
6	1	9	5	4	2	8	3	7
8	7	4	6	9	3	5	2	1
3	5	2	8	7	1	4	6	9
1	2	5	7	3	4	6	9	8
7	6	3	9	8	5	2	1	4
4	9	8	1	2	6	3	7	5

68

1	6	9	3	7	2	4	5	8
3	7	2	5	4	8	1	6	9
8	5	4	1	6	9	2	7	3
5	4	7	9	2	3	6	8	1
9	8	3	6	5	1	7	4	2
6	2	1	7	8	4	9	3	5
2	3	8	4	1	7	5	9	6
7	1	6	8	9	5	3	2	4
4	9	5	2	3	6	8	1	7

72

5	9	4	2	1	3	6	8	7
6	2	3	8	7	9	4	1	5
7	1	8	6	4	5	9	2	3
3	5	1	7	6	2	8	4	9
4	7	6	9	8	1	5	3	2
9	8	2	5	3	4	1	7	6
2	4	7	1	9	6	3	5	8
8	3	9	4	5	7	2	6	1
1	6	5	3	2	8	7	9	4

73

4	8	7	1	9	5	3	2	6
2	3	9	8	6	7	4	1	5
5	1	6	4	3	2	8	9	7
9	5	8	2	7	4	6	3	1
3	7	1	6	8	9	5	4	2
6	4	2	5	1	3	7	8	9
1	9	5	7	4	8	2	6	3
7	6	4	3	2	1	9	5	8
8	2	3	9	5	6	1	7	4

77

2	6	5	1	8	7	3	4	9
4	9	7	3	2	6	1	8	5
8	1	3	9	5	4	6	2	7
3	8	6	5	7	1	4	9	2
9	7	4	2	6	8	5	1	3
1	5	2	4	9	3	7	6	8
6	2	9	7	4	5	8	3	1
7	3	8	6	1	2	9	5	4
5	4	1	8	3	9	2	7	6

74

2	8	7	3	6	4	5	1	9
6	9	4	5	7	1	2	8	3
1	5	3	9	2	8	6	7	4
8	4	9	7	1	5	3	2	6
3	1	2	4	9	6	7	5	8
7	6	5	8	3	2	4	9	1
5	7	1	6	8	3	9	4	2
4	3	8	2	5	9	1	6	7
9	2	6	1	4	7	8	3	5

78

3	5	7	9	8	4	2	6	1
6	8	4	1	2	3	5	9	7
9	2	1	7	6	5	3	4	8
7	3	2	4	1	6	9	8	5
4	1	8	5	3	9	6	7	2
5	6	9	8	7	2	4	1	3
8	4	6	3	5	7	1	2	9
1	9	3	2	4	8	7	5	6
2	7	5	6	9	1	8	3	4

75

7	3	5	1	9	8	4	6	2
1	2	4	6	7	5	3	9	8
9	6	8	2	3	4	5	7	1
4	8	3	5	6	9	1	2	7
5	1	9	3	2	7	8	4	6
2	7	6	4	8	1	9	3	5
6	9	1	7	5	3	2	8	4
3	5	2	8	4	6	7	1	9
8	4	7	9	1	2	6	5	3

79

6	8	9	2	1	3	7	4	5
5	7	2	4	6	8	9	1	3
1	4	3	7	9	5	8	6	2
7	9	8	5	2	6	4	3	1
3	5	4	9	8	1	2	7	6
2	1	6	3	7	4	5	8	9
8	3	5	6	4	9	1	2	7
9	2	1	8	3	7	6	5	4
4	6	7	1	5	2	3	9	8

76

4	3	6	9	1	5	8	7	2
7	1	5	2	6	8	4	9	3
8	2	9	7	4	3	6	5	1
2	4	3	8	7	9	5	1	6
6	9	1	5	3	4	7	2	8
5	8	7	6	2	1	3	4	9
1	6	4	3	5	2	9	8	7
9	7	2	4	8	6	1	3	5
3	5	8	1	9	7	2	6	4

80

3	1	2	9	7	6	8	4	5
8	9	6	4	5	1	3	7	2
7	4	5	8	3	2	9	6	1
9	6	7	3	1	4	2	5	8
1	8	4	5	2	9	6	3	7
2	5	3	6	8	7	1	9	4
5	2	1	7	9	3	4	8	6
4	3	8	1	6	5	7	2	9
6	7	9	2	4	8	5	1	3

81

1	6	5	8	3	2	7	9	4
8	4	3	7	6	9	1	2	5
7	2	9	4	1	5	8	3	6
9	5	2	3	8	1	4	6	7
3	1	6	5	4	7	9	8	2
4	7	8	2	9	6	5	1	3
5	9	4	6	2	8	3	7	1
2	3	1	9	7	4	6	5	8
6	8	7	1	5	3	2	4	9

85

4	5	8	2	3	9	1	6	7
6	2	3	7	1	4	5	9	8
1	9	7	6	8	5	3	2	4
3	4	2	9	6	8	7	1	5
9	7	5	3	4	1	6	8	2
8	6	1	5	7	2	9	4	3
7	3	9	8	2	6	4	5	1
2	1	6	4	5	7	8	3	9
5	8	4	1	9	3	2	7	6

82

6	7	8	5	9	3	4	2	1
4	9	1	8	7	2	5	6	3
3	5	2	1	4	6	7	8	9
1	8	5	6	3	7	2	9	4
9	4	3	2	1	5	8	7	6
7	2	6	9	8	4	1	3	5
8	3	7	4	5	9	6	1	2
5	6	9	7	2	1	3	4	8
2	1	4	3	6	8	9	5	7

86

4	6	5	7	3	1	8	2	9
9	7	3	8	4	2	6	5	1
1	2	8	5	9	6	4	7	3
5	1	7	4	2	3	9	8	6
6	3	2	9	8	5	1	4	7
8	9	4	6	1	7	2	3	5
2	5	9	3	6	4	7	1	8
3	8	1	2	7	9	5	6	4
7	4	6	1	5	8	3	9	2

83

4	1	7	2	3	6	9	5	8
2	6	8	7	5	9	1	3	4
5	9	3	8	4	1	6	7	2
9	8	5	3	1	4	2	6	7
6	3	2	9	7	5	4	8	1
1	7	4	6	8	2	5	9	3
8	4	9	5	2	7	3	1	6
7	2	6	1	9	3	8	4	5
3	5	1	4	6	8	7	2	9

87

5	6	1	9	2	3	7	8	4
2	8	3	1	4	7	6	9	5
9	7	4	6	8	5	2	1	3
7	3	6	4	9	2	1	5	8
4	9	2	5	1	8	3	7	6
1	5	8	7	3	6	4	2	9
8	4	9	2	6	1	5	3	7
6	1	7	3	5	9	8	4	2
3	2	5	8	7	4	9	6	1

84

8	9	1	4	6	5	3	7	2
3	2	5	9	1	7	6	8	4
7	4	6	2	8	3	1	5	9
4	6	8	1	7	9	5	2	3
9	3	7	6	5	2	8	4	1
5	1	2	3	4	8	7	9	6
2	7	4	5	3	1	9	6	8
1	5	9	8	2	6	4	3	7
6	8	3	7	9	4	2	1	5

88

7	2	6	9	5	3	4	1	8
1	5	4	8	6	2	3	9	7
3	9	8	1	4	7	2	5	6
9	6	3	2	8	4	5	7	1
8	7	1	3	9	5	6	4	2
2	4	5	7	1	6	8	3	9
6	3	2	5	7	9	1	8	4
5	8	7	4	2	1	9	6	3
4	1	9	6	3	8	7	2	5

89

3	9	4	6	2	7	1	8	5
2	1	5	8	3	9	7	4	6
6	8	7	5	4	1	3	9	2
9	7	3	4	5	2	8	6	1
4	5	8	7	1	6	9	2	3
1	6	2	3	9	8	4	5	7
5	2	9	1	7	4	6	3	8
8	3	1	9	6	5	2	7	4
7	4	6	2	8	3	5	1	9

93

3	2	9	5	7	4	1	6	8
5	8	6	3	2	1	7	4	9
1	7	4	8	9	6	3	2	5
4	3	5	9	6	7	8	1	2
7	9	2	1	5	8	4	3	6
8	6	1	4	3	2	9	5	7
9	5	8	2	4	3	6	7	1
2	4	7	6	1	9	5	8	3
6	1	3	7	8	5	2	9	4

90

5	6	4	2	9	3	8	7	1
7	2	8	5	4	1	3	9	6
3	1	9	6	8	7	4	5	2
8	5	7	3	2	4	1	6	9
4	9	6	8	1	5	2	3	7
2	3	1	7	6	9	5	4	8
6	7	5	1	3	2	9	8	4
1	4	3	9	7	8	6	2	5
9	8	2	4	5	6	7	1	3

94

7	6	1	3	9	2	4	5	8
8	9	2	4	7	5	1	6	3
4	5	3	6	1	8	7	9	2
6	4	5	2	8	3	9	1	7
2	7	9	5	4	1	3	8	6
3	1	8	7	6	9	5	2	4
5	8	6	9	3	7	2	4	1
1	2	7	8	5	4	6	3	9
9	3	4	1	2	6	8	7	5

91

8	5	2	7	3	6	9	1	4
3	4	9	1	2	8	5	7	6
1	6	7	4	5	9	2	8	3
9	1	5	3	8	4	7	6	2
6	2	8	5	9	7	4	3	1
7	3	4	2	6	1	8	5	9
2	7	1	8	4	3	6	9	5
5	9	3	6	7	2	1	4	8
4	8	6	9	1	5	3	2	7

95

2	7	6	5	1	4	3	9	8
4	8	5	9	3	6	7	1	2
1	3	9	2	8	7	4	5	6
3	5	4	7	6	2	9	8	1
8	2	7	1	4	9	5	6	3
9	6	1	3	5	8	2	4	7
6	1	3	4	7	5	8	2	9
5	9	8	6	2	3	1	7	4
7	4	2	8	9	1	6	3	5

92

1	7	4	9	2	6	3	8	5
8	9	5	7	3	1	4	6	2
2	6	3	5	4	8	9	1	7
4	2	1	6	9	5	7	3	8
3	5	7	8	1	4	2	9	6
6	8	9	2	7	3	5	4	1
7	3	2	1	8	9	6	5	4
5	4	8	3	6	2	1	7	9
9	1	6	4	5	7	8	2	3

96

9	8	7	4	6	3	1	2	5
3	5	1	2	9	7	4	6	8
2	6	4	1	8	5	3	7	9
7	4	5	8	3	2	6	9	1
6	9	8	7	4	1	2	5	3
1	3	2	6	5	9	7	8	4
4	7	6	5	1	8	9	3	2
5	1	9	3	2	6	8	4	7
8	2	3	9	7	4	5	1	6

97

5	7	1	3	4	2	6	9	8
6	2	3	1	8	9	5	7	4
4	8	9	6	5	7	2	1	3
9	5	2	4	7	6	3	8	1
7	1	6	8	2	3	9	4	5
3	4	8	9	1	5	7	6	2
1	6	5	2	9	4	8	3	7
8	9	7	5	3	1	4	2	6
2	3	4	7	6	8	1	5	9

101

7	8	2	1	4	6	3	9	5
6	1	9	5	2	3	4	8	7
3	4	5	9	7	8	1	6	2
5	2	7	6	8	4	9	3	1
8	3	1	2	9	5	6	7	4
9	6	4	7	3	1	2	5	8
2	7	6	4	5	9	8	1	3
1	5	8	3	6	2	7	4	9
4	9	3	8	1	7	5	2	6

98

4	3	8	9	2	5	1	6	7
6	5	2	1	3	7	4	8	9
1	9	7	4	6	8	2	3	5
8	4	6	5	1	9	3	7	2
9	7	3	6	4	2	8	5	1
2	1	5	7	8	3	9	4	6
5	8	9	2	7	4	6	1	3
7	6	4	3	9	1	5	2	8
3	2	1	8	5	6	7	9	4

102

9	4	3	6	7	5	8	1	2
7	8	2	1	4	9	5	3	6
1	5	6	2	3	8	4	9	7
4	1	7	5	2	6	9	8	3
5	3	8	4	9	7	6	2	1
2	6	9	8	1	3	7	4	5
8	9	1	7	5	2	3	6	4
3	2	5	9	6	4	1	7	8
6	7	4	3	8	1	2	5	9

99

2	4	8	9	3	7	5	6	1
3	5	9	6	1	4	2	8	7
7	1	6	2	8	5	4	9	3
9	6	1	3	4	2	7	5	8
4	7	3	8	5	6	1	2	9
5	8	2	1	7	9	3	4	6
1	3	4	5	9	8	6	7	2
6	9	5	7	2	1	8	3	4
8	2	7	4	6	3	9	1	5

103

7	5	1	3	6	2	4	9	8
8	3	9	1	7	4	6	5	2
4	6	2	9	5	8	1	7	3
3	4	6	2	8	9	7	1	5
5	1	8	7	4	3	2	6	9
9	2	7	6	1	5	8	3	4
6	9	5	8	2	7	3	4	1
2	7	3	4	9	1	5	8	6
1	8	4	5	3	6	9	2	7

100

2	1	8	7	6	9	5	3	4
6	3	9	5	1	4	2	7	8
4	5	7	2	8	3	6	9	1
1	6	5	9	3	2	4	8	7
7	4	3	6	5	8	1	2	9
8	9	2	4	7	1	3	6	5
9	8	1	3	4	6	7	5	2
3	7	4	8	2	5	9	1	6
5	2	6	1	9	7	8	4	3

104

2	3	5	1	9	8	4	6	7
4	9	8	7	3	6	5	2	1
7	1	6	2	4	5	9	3	8
8	6	1	4	2	7	3	5	9
5	2	3	9	6	1	7	8	4
9	7	4	5	8	3	2	1	6
3	8	7	6	5	9	1	4	2
6	4	9	3	1	2	8	7	5
1	5	2	8	7	4	6	9	3

105

5	4	2	9	6	3	7	8	1
3	6	8	7	2	1	4	5	9
1	7	9	8	4	5	3	6	2
2	5	4	1	8	9	6	7	3
7	9	6	2	3	4	5	1	8
8	1	3	5	7	6	2	9	4
9	3	7	6	1	2	8	4	5
6	2	5	4	9	8	1	3	7
4	8	1	3	5	7	9	2	6

109

8	7	5	4	2	9	1	6	3
1	9	6	3	8	7	5	2	4
4	2	3	6	5	1	8	7	9
3	8	7	5	6	2	9	4	1
2	4	1	9	7	3	6	5	8
6	5	9	1	4	8	2	3	7
5	1	4	8	3	6	7	9	2
7	6	8	2	9	4	3	1	5
9	3	2	7	1	5	4	8	6

106

4	1	7	3	8	6	9	2	5
8	2	3	5	9	7	6	1	4
6	5	9	2	4	1	3	7	8
7	8	6	4	2	3	5	9	1
1	3	4	9	6	5	7	8	2
2	9	5	1	7	8	4	6	3
5	4	8	6	1	9	2	3	7
3	6	1	7	5	2	8	4	9
9	7	2	8	3	4	1	5	6

110

3	8	7	9	4	5	2	1	6
1	6	9	8	2	7	5	4	3
4	5	2	6	1	3	8	9	7
7	9	4	5	3	6	1	8	2
5	1	6	2	8	9	7	3	4
8	2	3	1	7	4	9	6	5
9	3	8	7	6	2	4	5	1
2	4	5	3	9	1	6	7	8
6	7	1	4	5	8	3	2	9

107

2	4	8	3	1	9	5	6	7
6	7	1	8	2	5	4	3	9
5	9	3	6	7	4	2	8	1
3	5	2	1	8	7	6	9	4
8	6	7	4	9	2	3	1	5
9	1	4	5	6	3	7	2	8
4	2	9	7	3	1	8	5	6
7	3	6	9	5	8	1	4	2
1	8	5	2	4	6	9	7	3

111

2	5	4	7	3	6	9	8	1
8	7	3	1	2	9	4	5	6
6	1	9	4	8	5	3	2	7
1	4	7	5	9	8	2	6	3
3	8	5	6	7	2	1	4	9
9	6	2	3	1	4	5	7	8
5	3	1	8	4	7	6	9	2
4	9	8	2	6	1	7	3	5
7	2	6	9	5	3	8	1	4

108

6	8	1	9	2	3	4	7	5
4	7	3	8	5	1	9	6	2
2	9	5	4	6	7	1	8	3
3	2	9	6	7	4	5	1	8
8	1	7	3	9	5	2	4	6
5	4	6	2	1	8	3	9	7
1	6	8	5	3	9	7	2	4
7	3	2	1	4	6	8	5	9
9	5	4	7	8	2	6	3	1

112

4	3	1	2	8	9	6	5	7
6	7	9	1	5	3	4	2	8
5	2	8	6	7	4	3	1	9
9	6	5	7	3	2	8	4	1
7	1	4	8	9	6	5	3	2
2	8	3	4	1	5	9	7	6
3	9	6	5	2	7	1	8	4
1	5	2	9	4	8	7	6	3
8	4	7	3	6	1	2	9	5

113

3	4	6	2	8	1	7	9	5
2	9	5	3	7	6	8	4	1
8	1	7	4	5	9	3	6	2
9	7	2	5	4	3	1	8	6
1	8	4	6	9	7	2	5	3
5	6	3	1	2	8	4	7	9
7	5	1	9	3	4	6	2	8
6	2	8	7	1	5	9	3	4
4	3	9	8	6	2	5	1	7

117

9	6	7	4	3	2	1	8	5
4	5	1	6	8	7	9	2	3
2	3	8	9	5	1	6	7	4
7	1	5	3	9	8	4	6	2
3	9	6	1	2	4	7	5	8
8	4	2	7	6	5	3	1	9
1	8	9	5	4	6	2	3	7
5	7	3	2	1	9	8	4	6
6	2	4	8	7	3	5	9	1

114

8	5	4	9	1	7	2	6	3
1	3	6	2	4	5	8	9	7
2	9	7	3	8	6	1	5	4
4	6	8	1	2	3	5	7	9
3	7	9	6	5	8	4	1	2
5	1	2	4	7	9	3	8	6
9	8	5	7	3	2	6	4	1
7	2	1	8	6	4	9	3	5
6	4	3	5	9	1	7	2	8

118

3	5	1	7	4	2	9	6	8
6	4	2	5	9	8	7	1	3
7	9	8	6	1	3	5	4	2
2	1	3	9	5	6	8	7	4
9	8	6	2	7	4	1	3	5
5	7	4	8	3	1	2	9	6
1	6	9	3	8	5	4	2	7
4	3	5	1	2	7	6	8	9
8	2	7	4	6	9	3	5	1

115

9	4	8	7	2	5	1	6	3
3	5	7	4	6	1	9	8	2
1	2	6	8	3	9	5	7	4
4	9	2	6	5	8	3	1	7
7	8	1	3	9	4	6	2	5
5	6	3	2	1	7	8	4	9
6	7	5	1	4	3	2	9	8
2	3	4	9	8	6	7	5	1
8	1	9	5	7	2	4	3	6

119

8	4	5	2	6	3	9	1	7
7	3	6	9	8	1	2	4	5
1	9	2	4	7	5	3	8	6
9	1	7	6	2	4	5	3	8
6	5	3	7	1	8	4	2	9
2	8	4	5	3	9	6	7	1
5	6	8	3	4	7	1	9	2
3	2	1	8	9	6	7	5	4
4	7	9	1	5	2	8	6	3

116

5	6	1	4	7	8	2	9	3
8	9	4	6	2	3	1	5	7
2	3	7	5	9	1	4	8	6
3	1	8	7	6	4	9	2	5
9	7	5	1	3	2	8	6	4
6	4	2	9	8	5	7	3	1
1	8	3	2	5	7	6	4	9
7	5	9	8	4	6	3	1	2
4	2	6	3	1	9	5	7	8

120

8	7	3	9	5	1	6	2	4
9	1	4	6	2	8	7	3	5
6	5	2	3	7	4	8	1	9
3	6	5	4	9	2	1	7	8
7	9	1	8	3	5	2	4	6
4	2	8	1	6	7	5	9	3
5	3	9	2	1	6	4	8	7
2	8	6	7	4	9	3	5	1
1	4	7	5	8	3	9	6	2

121

9	3	8	7	1	5	2	4	6
2	7	5	4	3	6	1	8	9
1	6	4	9	8	2	7	3	5
8	1	9	6	7	3	5	2	4
3	2	7	5	4	1	6	9	8
5	4	6	8	2	9	3	1	7
4	5	3	2	9	7	8	6	1
6	8	2	1	5	4	9	7	3
7	9	1	3	6	8	4	5	2

125

4	2	9	8	1	7	6	5	3
1	6	3	4	2	5	8	7	9
5	8	7	6	3	9	2	1	4
9	1	6	7	8	4	5	3	2
8	4	2	9	5	3	1	6	7
7	3	5	1	6	2	4	9	8
6	9	1	3	4	8	7	2	5
2	7	8	5	9	1	3	4	6
3	5	4	2	7	6	9	8	1

122

3	5	4	6	7	8	1	9	2
7	6	2	5	9	1	3	8	4
1	8	9	2	3	4	6	5	7
2	4	6	3	8	5	7	1	9
9	1	8	4	6	7	5	2	3
5	3	7	1	2	9	8	4	6
8	2	1	7	4	3	9	6	5
4	7	5	9	1	6	2	3	8
6	9	3	8	5	2	4	7	1

126

1	8	5	4	3	2	7	9	6
6	2	9	1	7	8	3	5	4
7	3	4	6	5	9	1	8	2
8	4	7	9	6	5	2	3	1
2	5	3	7	4	1	8	6	9
9	6	1	8	2	3	4	7	5
3	7	2	5	1	6	9	4	8
4	9	6	2	8	7	5	1	3
5	1	8	3	9	4	6	2	7

123

8	5	9	2	6	7	1	4	3
6	4	2	1	3	9	7	5	8
3	7	1	8	5	4	2	6	9
7	6	5	3	1	2	9	8	4
9	1	3	4	8	6	5	2	7
2	8	4	9	7	5	6	3	1
4	2	7	5	9	8	3	1	6
1	9	8	6	2	3	4	7	5
5	3	6	7	4	1	8	9	2

127

6	5	2	4	9	1	7	3	8
9	1	3	7	8	6	2	5	4
8	7	4	5	3	2	9	6	1
7	3	6	2	1	8	4	9	5
4	9	1	6	5	3	8	2	7
2	8	5	9	7	4	3	1	6
3	4	7	1	6	9	5	8	2
5	6	8	3	2	7	1	4	9
1	2	9	8	4	5	6	7	3

124

8	2	1	3	6	7	9	5	4
7	6	4	2	9	5	8	3	1
9	3	5	1	4	8	7	6	2
4	1	7	5	3	6	2	9	8
6	8	9	4	7	2	5	1	3
3	5	2	9	8	1	4	7	6
2	9	8	7	1	3	6	4	5
1	7	6	8	5	4	3	2	9
5	4	3	6	2	9	1	8	7

128

3	7	2	6	5	9	8	4	1
6	4	1	3	8	7	9	5	2
9	8	5	1	2	4	7	3	6
7	5	3	8	4	6	1	2	9
8	2	9	5	1	3	6	7	4
4	1	6	7	9	2	3	8	5
2	9	8	4	7	1	5	6	3
1	3	7	2	6	5	4	9	8
5	6	4	9	3	8	2	1	7

SOLUTIONS

129

7	4	3	5	1	9	8	2	6
8	2	9	3	4	6	1	7	5
5	1	6	7	2	8	9	3	4
4	7	2	8	3	5	6	9	1
6	3	5	1	9	4	7	8	2
1	9	8	2	6	7	4	5	3
3	8	7	4	5	1	2	6	9
2	6	1	9	8	3	5	4	7
9	5	4	6	7	2	3	1	8

133

3	2	8	9	6	4	1	7	5
7	5	6	2	8	1	9	4	3
9	1	4	3	7	5	2	6	8
5	4	1	7	3	2	6	8	9
8	3	2	6	5	9	4	1	7
6	9	7	4	1	8	3	5	2
2	8	3	1	4	7	5	9	6
4	7	9	5	2	6	8	3	1
1	6	5	8	9	3	7	2	4

130

8	5	4	3	1	6	9	7	2
7	2	3	5	4	9	6	1	8
1	6	9	7	8	2	5	4	3
2	3	7	1	6	8	4	5	9
4	9	6	2	3	5	1	8	7
5	8	1	4	9	7	2	3	6
9	7	8	6	5	4	3	2	1
3	4	2	9	7	1	8	6	5
6	1	5	8	2	3	7	9	4

134

2	5	4	8	3	9	1	7	6
7	9	3	4	1	6	8	2	5
6	1	8	2	7	5	3	9	4
9	2	1	6	5	8	7	4	3
3	4	5	7	9	1	6	8	2
8	6	7	3	2	4	9	5	1
1	8	6	5	4	7	2	3	9
4	3	9	1	8	2	5	6	7
5	7	2	9	6	3	4	1	8

131

1	2	9	4	6	8	3	5	7
4	6	5	3	1	7	2	8	9
3	7	8	2	5	9	6	4	1
2	9	4	5	3	1	7	6	8
7	1	6	9	8	4	5	2	3
5	8	3	7	2	6	9	1	4
6	3	1	8	7	2	4	9	5
9	5	2	1	4	3	8	7	6
8	4	7	6	9	5	1	3	2

135

1	5	3	4	9	2	8	7	6
7	4	9	8	1	6	2	3	5
2	8	6	3	7	5	4	1	9
3	6	2	9	4	7	1	5	8
8	9	7	6	5	1	3	4	2
4	1	5	2	8	3	6	9	7
5	7	8	1	6	4	9	2	3
6	2	4	7	3	9	5	8	1
9	3	1	5	2	8	7	6	4

132

4	8	3	9	7	1	5	2	6
2	6	1	4	8	5	7	9	3
7	9	5	2	3	6	8	4	1
9	3	2	8	1	7	4	6	5
6	1	7	5	9	4	3	8	2
8	5	4	6	2	3	9	1	7
5	7	8	1	6	9	2	3	4
3	2	6	7	4	8	1	5	9
1	4	9	3	5	2	6	7	8

136

8	9	7	4	3	1	2	6	5
3	1	2	9	6	5	7	8	4
4	5	6	2	7	8	1	9	3
5	6	3	8	1	7	4	2	9
7	2	1	5	9	4	8	3	6
9	4	8	3	2	6	5	1	7
2	3	5	7	8	9	6	4	1
1	7	9	6	4	2	3	5	8
6	8	4	1	5	3	9	7	2

137

2	1	5	6	3	8	4	9	7
6	7	4	5	1	9	3	2	8
8	3	9	2	7	4	1	6	5
7	4	8	1	6	2	9	5	3
1	9	2	4	5	3	7	8	6
3	5	6	9	8	7	2	4	1
9	8	1	7	2	5	6	3	4
4	6	3	8	9	1	5	7	2
5	2	7	3	4	6	8	1	9

141

9	2	6	4	1	5	7	8	3
5	4	3	8	7	9	6	2	1
1	7	8	6	3	2	9	4	5
2	8	5	7	4	6	3	1	9
7	6	1	3	9	8	2	5	4
4	3	9	2	5	1	8	7	6
3	9	2	5	8	4	1	6	7
6	1	4	9	2	7	5	3	8
8	5	7	1	6	3	4	9	2

138

4	7	2	8	5	6	1	3	9
1	3	9	7	4	2	8	5	6
6	5	8	1	3	9	2	7	4
3	2	1	9	6	8	7	4	5
5	4	6	3	7	1	9	2	8
9	8	7	5	2	4	3	6	1
7	9	3	4	1	5	6	8	2
8	6	4	2	9	7	5	1	3
2	1	5	6	8	3	4	9	7

142

3	2	5	6	1	8	7	9	4
4	1	7	2	5	9	3	6	8
9	6	8	3	4	7	5	1	2
2	4	9	5	3	6	8	7	1
7	8	6	9	2	1	4	5	3
1	5	3	7	8	4	9	2	6
8	7	2	1	9	3	6	4	5
6	3	1	4	7	5	2	8	9
5	9	4	8	6	2	1	3	7

139

7	6	5	4	1	8	9	3	2
8	9	1	2	3	5	7	6	4
3	4	2	7	6	9	1	5	8
4	2	9	1	5	3	8	7	6
1	8	7	9	2	6	3	4	5
6	5	3	8	7	4	2	1	9
2	3	8	6	4	7	5	9	1
5	1	4	3	9	2	6	8	7
9	7	6	5	8	1	4	2	3

143

8	6	3	1	9	7	4	2	5
4	1	7	2	3	5	6	8	9
2	9	5	4	8	6	7	1	3
3	8	1	6	5	4	9	7	2
7	4	6	3	2	9	8	5	1
5	2	9	7	1	8	3	4	6
6	3	8	5	4	2	1	9	7
9	7	2	8	6	1	5	3	4
1	5	4	9	7	3	2	6	8

140

4	3	5	7	8	9	2	6	1
6	9	8	4	2	1	7	5	3
2	1	7	5	3	6	9	4	8
7	4	1	9	6	3	8	2	5
9	8	3	2	1	5	6	7	4
5	2	6	8	4	7	3	1	9
1	6	4	3	7	8	5	9	2
3	7	9	1	5	2	4	8	6
8	5	2	6	9	4	1	3	7

144

7	1	9	8	3	4	6	2	5
6	2	8	7	5	1	3	9	4
3	5	4	9	6	2	1	7	8
8	6	3	5	1	7	2	4	9
5	7	2	4	9	3	8	1	6
4	9	1	2	8	6	5	3	7
9	4	6	3	2	8	7	5	1
1	3	5	6	7	9	4	8	2
2	8	7	1	4	5	9	6	3

145

4	3	6	1	9	2	5	8	7
8	9	2	3	5	7	1	6	4
7	5	1	6	8	4	9	3	2
1	6	5	7	3	9	4	2	8
2	4	3	8	6	5	7	1	9
9	8	7	4	2	1	6	5	3
6	2	4	5	7	8	3	9	1
5	1	9	2	4	3	8	7	6
3	7	8	9	1	6	2	4	5

149

5	4	7	6	1	8	3	2	9
9	1	8	4	3	2	7	5	6
2	3	6	5	9	7	1	4	8
4	8	1	7	6	3	5	9	2
6	5	3	9	2	1	8	7	4
7	2	9	8	5	4	6	1	3
1	6	5	3	4	9	2	8	7
3	7	4	2	8	5	9	6	1
8	9	2	1	7	6	4	3	5

146

2	5	6	9	1	7	4	8	3
4	9	8	6	3	2	5	1	7
3	7	1	5	4	8	2	6	9
7	1	3	2	5	9	6	4	8
5	6	2	7	8	4	3	9	1
8	4	9	3	6	1	7	2	5
9	2	5	8	7	6	1	3	4
1	8	7	4	2	3	9	5	6
6	3	4	1	9	5	8	7	2

150

1	2	9	4	6	8	3	7	5
4	8	5	3	2	7	1	6	9
6	7	3	1	5	9	4	2	8
2	6	4	5	1	3	9	8	7
9	1	8	2	7	4	5	3	6
5	3	7	8	9	6	2	1	4
8	5	6	9	3	2	7	4	1
7	9	2	6	4	1	8	5	3
3	4	1	7	8	5	6	9	2

147

8	4	9	1	2	5	6	3	7
1	2	7	8	6	3	4	9	5
3	6	5	9	7	4	2	1	8
4	9	6	7	5	1	8	2	3
7	1	8	6	3	2	9	5	4
5	3	2	4	9	8	1	7	6
2	8	1	5	4	7	3	6	9
9	7	4	3	1	6	5	8	2
6	5	3	2	8	9	7	4	1

151

5	9	4	2	8	6	1	3	7
1	6	7	5	3	9	2	4	8
2	8	3	4	1	7	5	6	9
4	3	5	8	2	1	9	7	6
9	2	6	7	4	5	8	1	3
7	1	8	6	9	3	4	5	2
8	5	1	3	6	2	7	9	4
3	7	2	9	5	4	6	8	1
6	4	9	1	7	8	3	2	5

148

6	3	1	9	2	4	8	7	5
7	9	5	1	6	8	3	2	4
8	4	2	5	3	7	9	6	1
9	2	7	4	1	3	5	8	6
3	5	6	7	8	9	4	1	2
4	1	8	2	5	6	7	3	9
1	6	9	8	7	5	2	4	3
5	7	3	6	4	2	1	9	8
2	8	4	3	9	1	6	5	7

152

4	6	1	7	9	8	3	5	2
7	3	8	2	5	6	4	9	1
5	2	9	1	4	3	8	7	6
6	9	4	3	8	5	1	2	7
2	5	3	6	1	7	9	4	8
1	8	7	9	2	4	5	6	3
3	1	6	4	7	9	2	8	5
8	4	2	5	6	1	7	3	9
9	7	5	8	3	2	6	1	4

153

9	7	2	6	8	3	4	1	5
1	8	4	5	7	9	6	3	2
3	5	6	2	4	1	7	9	8
6	3	5	8	1	4	9	2	7
4	2	1	9	5	7	3	8	6
7	9	8	3	2	6	1	5	4
8	1	3	7	6	5	2	4	9
2	4	7	1	9	8	5	6	3
5	6	9	4	3	2	8	7	1

157

5	2	4	9	6	8	7	3	1
3	9	7	1	4	5	6	2	8
6	1	8	3	2	7	9	5	4
1	7	2	4	9	6	5	8	3
8	5	3	7	1	2	4	9	6
4	6	9	5	8	3	1	7	2
7	8	5	6	3	1	2	4	9
2	4	6	8	7	9	3	1	5
9	3	1	2	5	4	8	6	7

154

8	5	6	4	3	7	2	9	1
3	2	4	9	1	5	8	6	7
1	7	9	6	2	8	5	4	3
7	6	8	1	5	9	4	3	2
2	4	1	3	7	6	9	8	5
5	9	3	8	4	2	7	1	6
9	3	2	7	8	1	6	5	4
4	8	5	2	6	3	1	7	9
6	1	7	5	9	4	3	2	8

158

4	1	2	9	7	8	5	6	3
8	9	5	2	3	6	1	7	4
6	7	3	1	4	5	8	9	2
7	5	1	6	2	4	9	3	8
3	4	6	8	9	7	2	5	1
2	8	9	5	1	3	6	4	7
1	2	4	7	5	9	3	8	6
9	3	8	4	6	1	7	2	5
5	6	7	3	8	2	4	1	9

155

1	3	5	6	8	9	4	7	2
7	9	2	5	1	4	3	6	8
8	6	4	3	2	7	1	9	5
5	1	7	9	3	2	8	4	6
3	2	6	8	4	1	9	5	7
9	4	8	7	5	6	2	3	1
4	7	1	2	6	3	5	8	9
2	8	9	4	7	5	6	1	3
6	5	3	1	9	8	7	2	4

159

1	2	7	3	6	5	8	9	4
5	4	3	2	8	9	6	1	7
8	9	6	7	4	1	3	2	5
2	3	1	4	7	6	9	5	8
9	6	8	5	1	3	4	7	2
4	7	5	8	9	2	1	3	6
3	8	2	1	5	4	7	6	9
6	5	4	9	3	7	2	8	1
7	1	9	6	2	8	5	4	3

156

2	6	9	5	8	1	4	3	7
3	7	1	2	4	6	9	5	8
4	5	8	7	9	3	1	6	2
9	2	3	4	6	8	7	1	5
1	4	5	9	2	7	3	8	6
6	8	7	3	1	5	2	9	4
5	1	2	8	3	4	6	7	9
7	3	4	6	5	9	8	2	1
8	9	6	1	7	2	5	4	3

160

4	1	6	9	7	3	8	5	2
5	2	9	8	1	6	4	3	7
3	7	8	2	5	4	6	9	1
1	6	3	4	9	5	7	2	8
7	8	5	3	2	1	9	6	4
2	9	4	7	6	8	3	1	5
6	5	7	1	8	9	2	4	3
9	3	2	5	4	7	1	8	6
8	4	1	6	3	2	5	7	9

SOLUTIONS

161

9	1	4	5	8	3	2	7	6
7	5	3	1	6	2	8	4	9
6	2	8	4	7	9	1	3	5
5	3	6	8	2	4	9	1	7
4	8	1	7	9	5	3	6	2
2	7	9	6	3	1	5	8	4
3	9	7	2	4	8	6	5	1
1	4	2	3	5	6	7	9	8
8	6	5	9	1	7	4	2	3

165

8	9	2	7	1	4	6	5	3
5	1	6	9	8	3	4	2	7
4	7	3	6	2	5	1	8	9
9	2	1	5	3	6	8	7	4
7	3	8	1	4	9	2	6	5
6	4	5	8	7	2	9	3	1
2	6	9	4	5	7	3	1	8
1	5	4	3	6	8	7	9	2
3	8	7	2	9	1	5	4	6

162

8	2	7	9	6	3	1	5	4
4	3	6	5	8	1	2	9	7
9	1	5	7	4	2	6	3	8
5	8	2	3	9	7	4	6	1
6	9	3	2	1	4	8	7	5
7	4	1	6	5	8	3	2	9
3	7	4	1	2	9	5	8	6
1	5	9	8	3	6	7	4	2
2	6	8	4	7	5	9	1	3

166

1	6	7	4	3	8	9	2	5
4	3	2	6	9	5	8	7	1
8	5	9	1	2	7	6	3	4
3	9	1	2	8	6	5	4	7
6	7	8	5	4	1	3	9	2
5	2	4	3	7	9	1	8	6
9	8	6	7	1	2	4	5	3
2	4	5	8	6	3	7	1	9
7	1	3	9	5	4	2	6	8

163

1	3	2	7	5	4	8	6	9
5	4	9	8	6	1	7	2	3
8	6	7	2	9	3	1	5	4
2	1	6	9	3	5	4	8	7
4	8	3	1	7	2	5	9	6
9	7	5	4	8	6	2	3	1
3	5	1	6	4	8	9	7	2
7	2	8	3	1	9	6	4	5
6	9	4	5	2	7	3	1	8

167

3	9	2	8	4	6	7	5	1
7	5	4	1	2	9	3	6	8
6	1	8	3	7	5	4	2	9
8	2	1	4	5	3	9	7	6
9	4	7	2	6	8	5	1	3
5	3	6	9	1	7	8	4	2
2	8	5	6	9	4	1	3	7
4	6	3	7	8	1	2	9	5
1	7	9	5	3	2	6	8	4

164

4	7	2	8	9	6	5	3	1
1	3	8	4	5	7	2	9	6
5	9	6	3	1	2	4	7	8
9	1	5	6	2	8	3	4	7
8	2	3	7	4	1	6	5	9
7	6	4	5	3	9	8	1	2
6	4	1	9	8	5	7	2	3
3	8	9	2	7	4	1	6	5
2	5	7	1	6	3	9	8	4

168

1	3	5	9	6	7	4	8	2
4	2	9	1	8	5	3	7	6
6	8	7	4	3	2	1	9	5
8	5	6	7	1	9	2	4	3
2	7	1	3	4	6	9	5	8
9	4	3	5	2	8	6	1	7
3	1	8	6	5	4	7	2	9
7	6	2	8	9	1	5	3	4
5	9	4	2	7	3	8	6	1

169

7	3	1	9	8	5	6	4	2
6	2	5	3	1	4	8	7	9
4	9	8	6	2	7	5	1	3
5	7	2	8	4	6	9	3	1
1	6	9	2	7	3	4	5	8
8	4	3	1	5	9	7	2	6
3	5	6	7	9	2	1	8	4
2	8	4	5	6	1	3	9	7
9	1	7	4	3	8	2	6	5

173

4	9	2	8	3	6	5	7	1
3	7	6	1	5	4	2	8	9
1	5	8	9	7	2	4	3	6
5	1	7	6	2	9	8	4	3
6	3	9	5	4	8	7	1	2
2	8	4	3	1	7	9	6	5
8	4	1	2	6	5	3	9	7
7	2	3	4	9	1	6	5	8
9	6	5	7	8	3	1	2	4

170

8	6	2	5	9	7	1	4	3
3	5	9	6	4	1	8	2	7
1	7	4	8	2	3	9	5	6
6	3	7	1	8	2	5	9	4
4	2	1	9	6	5	7	3	8
9	8	5	7	3	4	2	6	1
5	9	6	3	1	8	4	7	2
2	1	3	4	7	9	6	8	5
7	4	8	2	5	6	3	1	9

174

2	8	1	9	4	6	7	3	5
9	3	6	2	7	5	8	1	4
7	4	5	8	1	3	9	6	2
8	9	7	3	5	1	2	4	6
4	5	2	6	9	7	1	8	3
6	1	3	4	8	2	5	7	9
5	2	4	7	6	8	3	9	1
3	6	8	1	2	9	4	5	7
1	7	9	5	3	4	6	2	8

171

8	9	7	1	4	3	5	2	6
4	2	5	7	6	8	3	1	9
1	3	6	9	5	2	8	4	7
9	8	1	3	2	4	7	6	5
3	5	4	6	9	7	2	8	1
6	7	2	5	8	1	9	3	4
2	1	8	4	7	9	6	5	3
5	4	9	8	3	6	1	7	2
7	6	3	2	1	5	4	9	8

175

6	2	1	9	7	5	8	3	4
9	5	4	3	6	8	7	2	1
3	8	7	2	4	1	6	5	9
5	4	3	7	8	6	9	1	2
1	6	9	5	2	3	4	7	8
8	7	2	4	1	9	5	6	3
4	3	5	6	9	2	1	8	7
2	9	8	1	5	7	3	4	6
7	1	6	8	3	4	2	9	5

172

2	1	6	3	5	7	9	4	8
7	8	3	1	4	9	5	2	6
4	9	5	6	8	2	1	7	3
9	2	8	7	6	3	4	1	5
3	6	1	4	9	5	7	8	2
5	4	7	2	1	8	6	3	9
8	3	4	5	7	6	2	9	1
1	5	2	9	3	4	8	6	7
6	7	9	8	2	1	3	5	4

176

4	3	8	9	7	6	5	2	1
2	9	7	1	4	5	8	3	6
6	1	5	8	2	3	7	4	9
1	8	9	3	5	2	4	6	7
7	2	3	6	9	4	1	8	5
5	6	4	7	1	8	3	9	2
3	7	1	2	8	9	6	5	4
8	5	2	4	6	1	9	7	3
9	4	6	5	3	7	2	1	8

177

3	5	6	1	2	7	8	4	9
1	2	9	6	4	8	7	3	5
7	8	4	5	3	9	6	1	2
2	4	5	7	8	1	9	6	3
8	9	1	3	6	5	2	7	4
6	7	3	4	9	2	1	5	8
5	3	8	2	7	6	4	9	1
9	1	7	8	5	4	3	2	6
4	6	2	9	1	3	5	8	7

181

4	2	7	8	3	1	9	6	5
3	6	8	5	9	7	1	2	4
1	5	9	6	4	2	8	7	3
7	3	1	4	6	8	5	9	2
2	8	4	9	1	5	7	3	6
6	9	5	2	7	3	4	1	8
5	4	3	1	2	9	6	8	7
8	1	2	7	5	6	3	4	9
9	7	6	3	8	4	2	5	1

178

7	9	8	4	2	6	1	5	3
1	2	5	7	3	9	8	4	6
6	4	3	1	8	5	9	2	7
2	5	6	9	1	3	4	7	8
8	7	1	2	6	4	5	3	9
4	3	9	5	7	8	2	6	1
9	8	7	6	5	2	3	1	4
3	1	2	8	4	7	6	9	5
5	6	4	3	9	1	7	8	2

182

2	6	9	4	5	1	7	8	3
7	4	5	6	3	8	1	9	2
8	3	1	2	9	7	5	6	4
6	9	4	1	2	5	8	3	7
1	7	3	8	6	9	4	2	5
5	8	2	3	7	4	6	1	9
3	2	7	5	8	6	9	4	1
9	1	6	7	4	2	3	5	8
4	5	8	9	1	3	2	7	6

179

4	7	3	8	2	9	1	6	5
1	9	8	5	6	3	2	7	4
6	2	5	1	7	4	3	8	9
2	8	1	4	9	5	6	3	7
5	3	7	6	1	2	9	4	8
9	4	6	7	3	8	5	2	1
8	1	4	3	5	6	7	9	2
7	6	9	2	8	1	4	5	3
3	5	2	9	4	7	8	1	6

183

1	4	7	6	2	3	9	5	8
9	5	8	1	7	4	6	2	3
3	2	6	8	9	5	4	7	1
6	1	5	4	3	2	7	8	9
7	8	3	9	6	1	5	4	2
4	9	2	7	5	8	3	1	6
2	3	9	5	8	7	1	6	4
5	6	4	2	1	9	8	3	7
8	7	1	3	4	6	2	9	5

180

7	5	8	9	4	1	2	6	3
1	4	6	5	3	2	9	7	8
3	2	9	7	6	8	5	4	1
6	7	3	8	1	9	4	5	2
5	9	4	3	2	7	1	8	6
2	8	1	4	5	6	3	9	7
4	1	2	6	8	5	7	3	9
8	3	7	2	9	4	6	1	5
9	6	5	1	7	3	8	2	4

184

6	8	4	1	2	5	9	3	7
1	5	7	8	9	3	6	2	4
9	3	2	4	6	7	1	5	8
3	9	8	7	5	2	4	1	6
2	1	6	9	4	8	3	7	5
4	7	5	3	1	6	2	8	9
8	4	3	6	7	1	5	9	2
7	2	9	5	3	4	8	6	1
5	6	1	2	8	9	7	4	3

185

9	1	4	7	3	2	5	6	8
5	2	3	6	8	9	1	4	7
8	7	6	4	1	5	3	2	9
3	6	5	9	4	8	2	7	1
1	8	7	2	6	3	9	5	4
4	9	2	5	7	1	8	3	6
6	3	8	1	5	4	7	9	2
2	4	1	3	9	7	6	8	5
7	5	9	8	2	6	4	1	3

189

4	9	8	2	3	1	7	6	5
2	5	7	8	6	9	1	4	3
3	1	6	7	4	5	8	9	2
6	7	1	9	5	3	4	2	8
9	4	2	1	7	8	3	5	6
5	8	3	4	2	6	9	1	7
8	3	4	5	9	2	6	7	1
1	2	9	6	8	7	5	3	4
7	6	5	3	1	4	2	8	9

186

7	8	2	5	4	1	9	3	6
1	4	6	8	3	9	2	7	5
3	5	9	2	7	6	4	1	8
2	7	8	1	9	3	6	5	4
6	1	4	7	2	5	8	9	3
9	3	5	6	8	4	1	2	7
4	9	7	3	1	8	5	6	2
8	6	3	9	5	2	7	4	1
5	2	1	4	6	7	3	8	9

190

8	6	1	5	3	2	9	7	4
7	5	9	6	4	8	1	2	3
4	2	3	9	7	1	5	6	8
3	4	5	2	1	9	7	8	6
2	9	7	8	6	4	3	1	5
6	1	8	3	5	7	4	9	2
1	7	2	4	8	5	6	3	9
9	3	4	1	2	6	8	5	7
5	8	6	7	9	3	2	4	1

187

7	8	6	4	3	9	5	2	1
4	1	2	5	7	6	8	3	9
9	5	3	8	1	2	4	6	7
1	7	4	2	6	8	3	9	5
2	6	9	7	5	3	1	4	8
8	3	5	1	9	4	2	7	6
6	9	1	3	2	5	7	8	4
3	4	7	9	8	1	6	5	2
5	2	8	6	4	7	9	1	3

191

3	4	2	5	6	1	8	9	7
9	8	5	7	4	3	6	1	2
1	6	7	2	9	8	3	4	5
8	7	6	9	1	2	4	5	3
2	5	1	4	3	7	9	6	8
4	3	9	8	5	6	2	7	1
6	2	8	1	7	4	5	3	9
5	1	4	3	2	9	7	8	6
7	9	3	6	8	5	1	2	4

188

7	9	6	2	8	4	3	5	1
3	2	4	7	5	1	9	8	6
8	5	1	3	9	6	2	4	7
5	7	2	6	4	9	8	1	3
6	8	9	5	1	3	7	2	4
4	1	3	8	2	7	5	6	9
2	4	7	1	3	5	6	9	8
9	3	5	4	6	8	1	7	2
1	6	8	9	7	2	4	3	5

192

8	5	7	1	3	2	6	9	4
3	1	4	6	7	9	5	2	8
9	6	2	8	4	5	3	1	7
5	3	9	2	8	4	1	7	6
6	7	8	3	9	1	4	5	2
4	2	1	7	5	6	8	3	9
2	4	3	9	1	8	7	6	5
1	9	5	4	6	7	2	8	3
7	8	6	5	2	3	9	4	1

SOLUTIONS

193

3	5	1	4	6	8	2	7	9
7	6	8	9	5	2	3	1	4
4	2	9	1	3	7	8	6	5
1	9	4	2	7	5	6	8	3
6	7	2	3	8	9	4	5	1
5	8	3	6	1	4	9	2	7
8	4	6	5	9	1	7	3	2
9	3	5	7	2	6	1	4	8
2	1	7	8	4	3	5	9	6

197

2	3	1	7	9	6	4	8	5
4	9	8	2	5	1	7	3	6
7	5	6	8	3	4	9	1	2
1	2	9	5	7	8	3	6	4
3	6	7	9	4	2	8	5	1
5	8	4	6	1	3	2	7	9
9	4	5	3	6	7	1	2	8
6	7	2	1	8	9	5	4	3
8	1	3	4	2	5	6	9	7

194

5	6	8	1	7	2	9	3	4
7	1	9	8	4	3	2	5	6
4	3	2	9	5	6	7	8	1
3	7	1	4	2	9	5	6	8
9	8	6	3	1	5	4	7	2
2	4	5	6	8	7	3	1	9
8	5	7	2	9	1	6	4	3
1	9	3	5	6	4	8	2	7
6	2	4	7	3	8	1	9	5

198

5	6	8	3	1	7	4	9	2
7	2	1	5	9	4	3	6	8
4	9	3	6	2	8	5	7	1
1	4	2	8	3	9	7	5	6
8	5	6	4	7	2	9	1	3
3	7	9	1	6	5	2	8	4
2	1	5	9	4	6	8	3	7
9	3	7	2	8	1	6	4	5
6	8	4	7	5	3	1	2	9

195

9	6	7	2	3	8	1	5	4
5	1	8	4	6	7	2	3	9
2	4	3	5	1	9	6	8	7
6	7	9	1	8	3	4	2	5
8	3	5	6	4	2	7	9	1
1	2	4	7	9	5	3	6	8
3	5	6	8	7	1	9	4	2
7	9	2	3	5	4	8	1	6
4	8	1	9	2	6	5	7	3

199

2	8	1	3	4	7	5	9	6
5	9	7	6	8	2	4	3	1
6	4	3	9	1	5	2	7	8
3	1	5	8	2	4	9	6	7
9	2	4	7	6	3	1	8	5
7	6	8	5	9	1	3	4	2
1	3	2	4	7	6	8	5	9
8	5	6	2	3	9	7	1	4
4	7	9	1	5	8	6	2	3

196

2	1	5	4	7	9	6	3	8
3	6	9	5	8	1	4	7	2
4	7	8	2	6	3	9	5	1
8	3	1	6	9	4	5	2	7
5	4	2	1	3	7	8	9	6
6	9	7	8	5	2	3	1	4
7	8	4	3	2	5	1	6	9
9	5	6	7	1	8	2	4	3
1	2	3	9	4	6	7	8	5

200

4	7	2	8	3	9	1	5	6
9	1	3	7	6	5	8	2	4
5	8	6	1	2	4	7	3	9
7	5	9	4	8	2	6	1	3
2	4	1	6	7	3	5	9	8
6	3	8	5	9	1	4	7	2
8	2	4	3	5	7	9	6	1
3	6	7	9	1	8	2	4	5
1	9	5	2	4	6	3	8	7